# Transition to a New Era

Neohumanism
Publications

# Transition to a
# New Era

Ronald Logan

**Neohumanism Publications**
356 Horn Lane
Eugene, Oregon 97404



Cover art by Asha Logan

Printed in USA
Printed by Kindle Direct Publishing

ISBN: 9798335312196

Some contents of this book originally appeared in the book, *PROUT: A New Paradigm of Development*. Other contents appeared as articles in the magazine, *PROUT*, published in New Delhi, India. All of the contents are inspired by the teachings of P.R. Sarkar as expressed by Maetreyii Nolan, Marc Nevas, and Ronald Logan.

# Contents

# 1

## The Need for a New Social Vision

There is an urgent need to replace the prevailing approach to socioeconomic development. So long as this is not done, humanity will face crises of increasing severity. The pace at which imbalances in the society are destabilizing the world is quickening. Reforms, while helpful, are insufficient to stem the tide; fundamental change is required. Capitalism's approach of centralizing economic power, maximizing profits, unsustainably plundering resources, and privileging individual gain at collective expense must be replaced with a new economic system that relocalizes economic control, uses resources sustainably, balances profits with care for the Earth and its people, and harmonizes individual gain with collective well-being.

Many people are aware that the capitalist system is disrupting planetary life. Out of this awareness has come an upwelling of new thinking and new social practices that are based on equity, inclusion, cooperation, decentralization, and regeneration. But what is lacking is a synthetic social vision that is grounded in an expansive understanding of human potentials and that offers a pathway to give it birth.

Many observers have analyzed the failures and costs of economic globalism and neoliberalism. The bad fruits of this world system are increasingly apparent. It's now time to bring forward ambitious efforts to establish and vitalize localized development based on new values and guided by a new social vision.

## An Integrated Framework for Change

The work of building local economies that can sustainably and equitably provide people's necessities needs to be undertaken in an *integrated framework* that gives attention to the following essential arenas of transformation:

First, articulating a *guiding socioeconomic theory*—the values, principles, and operating systems—of decentralized, equitable and sustainable development.

Second, developing *public policy guidelines and institutional frameworks* that support implementation of the new social vision.

Third, demonstrating and refining *operating models* of sustainable, integrated local development that inspire people with practical examples of new possibilities.

Fourth, providing *education*—trainings, publications, videos, social media content, etc.—to the early adopters of the new social vision and of its practice.

Fifth, organizing *social and electoral movements*, as needed, to raise grassroots calls for economic democracy so that local communities can be empowered to establish a progressive new system of socioeconomic development.

Each of these arenas of work are facets of a whole, and their respective contributions will have most effect if expressed in a movement for change that embraces them *as an integrated strategy, operating on multiple fronts.*

This will be challenging. Social theorists, policy wonks, model builders, educators and political activists generally inhabit independent realms, they are motivated by different passions, and they lack the vision to link their work with efforts in the other arenas. Connecting and linking these realms is the work of a visionary few whose minds can embrace a synthetic outlook. The nature of the social change that is needed requires as much coordination and collaboration as possible. Amidst the diverse expressions of people's impulse for transformation, there must be unity of purpose.

Of these five arenas of transformative work, the arena least amenable to coordination with the others is that of social movements. Grass-roots political action tends to ride the upwellings of sentiments that stir people to take action. Social movements are characterized by an immediacy and spontaneity that give them an independent dynamic. But the role of these movements is essential. There are those who think that introducing new ideas and demonstrating new models are sufficient to build a new society, but this is naive thinking. There is also need for the forceful political demands of the masses to propel institutional change.

## Global Metacrisis

People are understandably reticent to undertake fundamental change. However much care may be taken to guide an orderly transition to a new system, some disruption is inevitable. Also, change will be met with resistance. Most people who have a privileged position will not voluntarily relinquish their wealth and privilege, so the need for a new socioeconomic system must be compelling. People must realize that there is no choice, that the costs of continuing on are too great, and that, in the end, a suitable new system can provide a much better quality of life to all.

What will ultimately compel us to action? It will be the convergence of several crises that have capacity to bring massive disruption to society as we've known it. Each alone could have devastating consequences; together their threat is magnified.

**Resource depletion.** As world population continues to grow, resource use has grown even faster. Essential resources are now being depleted at an unsustainable rate. Resources are being used at such a rate that about 1.8 earths would be required to sustain humanity at the present level of resource use. Humanity has overshot the earth's carrying capacity.

**Climate change.** Due to human created greenhouse gasses, Earth's climate is rapidly changing. Average annual temperatures have risen steadily, as has the frequency of extreme weather events. There is a real possibility that the global climate system is close to tipping-points, which would bring a sudden shift in the stable climate humanity has enjoyed for the past twelve millennia.

**Environmental degradation.** Species are going extinct at a rate not seen since the fall of the dinosaurs. Earth is experiencing its sixth mass extinction event. As the destruction of the earth proceeds—consuming soils, aquifers, surface waters, coral reefs, forests, flood plain buffers, ecosystem biodiversity—the economic potentials of humanity are diminishing along with it.

**Economic crisis.** The two underlying causes of economic depressions are (1) the over-concentration of wealth among the rich, which reduces the purchasing capacity of the common people to the point that consumer demand is depressed, and (2) stagnancy in the movement of money in the productive economy, as investors withhold credit, or as investments are concentrated in non-productive speculation. Both conditions exist in the current global economy. While the number of billionaires grows, the real wages of the middle and lower classes lags. And excessive investments flow into speculative markets, where they are of little productive use and create the potential for financial instability.

These crises are not independent of each other; they are the acute symptoms of a larger metacrisis caused by a greed-driven economic system. They are interrelated, with the capacity to interact in complex and mutually reinforcing ways. As the effects of the global metacrisis intensify, and as they come together in perfect storm situations, disaster and hardship will become commonplace. Even where the hardships are not severe people will face dwindling possibilities to advance. The sinking ship of neoliberal capitalism must be abandoned, and the transition to a new society embraced.

Change—fundamental change—will not be easy. But its necessity is upon us. We can fail to act, at great cost to humanity's wellbeing, or accept the challenges and embrace promising new possibilities that are emerging.

Establishing a new modality of socioeconomic development—one that is decentralized, sustainable, inclusive, equitable, cooperative, and post-materialist—will require engagement, commitment, unity and leadership. And it will require a viable new social vision that can return balance to the society and unleash the suppressed potential of the human race.

## PROUT

The ideas offered in this book are based on the Progressive Utilization Theory (PROUT). PROUT is a social philosophy that is based in spirituality. This spirituality is characterized as a perennial or fundamental spirituality. It is not the spirituality of any sectarian path or spiritual movement but is a universal spirituality that acknowledges the wholeness and sacredness of being and that foregrounds the enduring values of love, compassion, service and reverence.

# 2

# Local Development and Global Confederation

In the world today there are difficulties that cannot be mitigated merely by good intentions. The situation with the world economy is fragile. Climate change is speeding up. There is growing scarcity of oil. The planet is being poisoned by pollution. Many ecosystems are under great stress. And there is increasing limitation in the planet's availability of resources to sustain the human population.

When one puts all of these together, it does not take great insight to recognize that humanity faces an increasingly imminent crisis. The lifestyle that has been normalized in this era is not sustainable; the amount of energy required to maintain the comforts of day-to-day life is not sustainable; and the ever-growing population is not sustainable. The earth simply cannot support so many people, living by current lifestyle standards.

What to do? One can say: "Everyone should cut down their energy use and minimize driving cars." But, realistically, will this happen? Will most abandon their cars and walk? Or not travel in airplanes? Such a solution will not happen.

It is more likely that the drive for survival will lead to viable alternative energy sources. Unfortunately, new energy sources will not be put in place soon enough, so there will inevitably be a tough time ahead. Humanity will have to face the climate changes caused by excessive population and the lifestyles that have been adopted. This cannot be avoided.

Clearly there are troubles ahead, and these troubles are converging. Aware people recognize that there is a problem; many heads of state know there is problem. And it is known that the problem will get very serious. Some say: "If there were alternative energies, the major problems could be controlled." A nice idea, but is it fully practical? By the time it is implemented, it will be too late. So we have to think, what to do?

## Local Development

Before there can be material solutions, there must be ideological solutions. If no one has an ideological framework suitable to work with the situation, it will only become more critical. Neohumanism and PROUT provide a very practical ideological framework. The PROUT approach to development emphasizes local, sustainable development. This emphasis on local economic development and sustainability will become critical in the coming years. As the global situation becomes more unstable, it will be essential that local communities be able to provide viable local solutions for the plight of their populations.

Without this capacity, who will people turn to when crises arise? If there are major disasters, if the economy is in crisis, if there are worldwide struggles, is there any national or international force that can be relied upon to solve these problems? Most nations are already challenged by the problems at hand. They will be overwhelmed by what the future situation brings. The need for local ability to handle difficulties and provide basic necessities is very great. For this, local development must be encouraged.

## An Empowered World Body

At the same time, there is a need to encourage the development of a confederation of nations, a world confederation which can exercise international power for the welfare of all people—not for corporate development, not for any group-centered purpose, but for the welfare of the peoples who inhabit the planet.

The lack of an empowered world body will be a critical concern in the coming years because, without this, how can the unsustainable global situation be addressed? Humanity faces growing global problems, but who is there to address it? Who has the authority and the power to speak for the entire planet, for the global society? At present, no one has.

There is a lack of global authority, and with this lack of authority two things will happen. First, those who have an exploiting nature will take opportunistic advantage of the situation, as many large corporate entities have already done. They will move in opportunistically to fill the gap. That is one result.

The second result is that no one will have the ability to cope with the difficulties and emergencies. The opportunists and corporations are not going to do it. They are not really interested in running the planet, in helping humanity survive. Their interest is to take advantage and to exploit.

So, on the one hand there are the corporate opportunists who take advantage and exploit, and on the other hand there is the lack of anyone to effectively manage the situation. There is a great need for a planetary authority to step into a global management role. This body must be representative of the entire planet; it must be a type of confederation. The United Nations is an initial attempt at providing global authority. But its authority is inadequate, and it is not truly representative.

There was a time when feudalism dominated much of the world. This monarch had his little territory, and that monarch had his territory. Then, with the rise of nationalism, the feudal kingdoms were consolidated into larger territories called nation-states. Now the nation-states cannot cope with planet-wide problems, and there is need for a global body to give leadership. Otherwise there will continue to be crises and opportunism.

A nation-state is no more dictatorial than a feudal state, and a world government will be no more dictatorial than a nation-state. But it will be capable of imposing a type of order that is desperately needed. What is required is not a world dictatorship, but a world body to establish a suitable structure for our globalized world.

The United Nations sees all of these problems, and it makes efforts to respond. But it has no authority, or its authority is dim. It can't effectively manage the problems. What authority does the United Nations have over the large multinational corporations? Or over the nations that support corporate exploitation? Their word must have force, and if their word is not listened to, they must be able to impose it upon states that will not comply.

Regulation on the planetary level will be the duty of the representative global body. Proper regulation of the global economy, of equitable distribution of resources, of corporate polluters, of currency stability, etc. cannot be assured so long as nations enjoy sovereign power, rather than this power being held by a global body.

And so long as the currently constituted United Nations has no independent military forces of its own, how can rogue nations be brought into alignment? How can planetary peace be maintained? It cannot. Those who have the power will do as they will.

And if they prefer to be aggressive, they will. Or if they prefer to use their influence in support of corporate opportunists, they can. This must turn around.

Both of these core elements of the PROUTist vision must be implemented: That is, there must be the emphasis on local development, and there must be the formation of a global confederation. Necessity will eventually cause the implementation of both of these approaches. But if these ideas can be made available to and accepted by humanity in a timely way, it will greatly ease the times ahead.

## The Future is Bright

This is a transition time in human history; an evolutionary jump is occurring. There is bound to be struggle and difficulty in the course of this transformation. But in essence it is a positive process, and the end results are bound to be good. In the era to come, the global human society will become closely bonded—this is its only way forward.

The future of humanity is bright. Even though there will be difficulties, there will be a bright side to it. Just as it is difficult to break a strong addiction in personal life, it is the same in collective life. Society is being forced to face its addiction to an unsustainable way of living. It may seem like things are falling apart, but what is occurring is that corrective measures are being forced upon us.

This crisis humanity now faces is an opportunity for people to come together to build community at the local level and a one-world society at the global level. With the establishment of one world society, many advances in human life will unfold. A very different world will arise. It is a great destiny to advance this change, to take part in this dynamic shift in humanity's evolution.

# 3

# Socioeconomic Development and Meeting Human Needs

Society should have as its highest goal the full physical, mental, and spiritual development of all its members. It should provide for the optimum development of all. If a society does this, then its members will have no artificial obstacles to their evolution and personal development, and they will have full opportunity to become true and noble human beings.

So, when a society is properly directed, properly focused, it can enhance the life of all of its members, which in turn leads to the health of the society. A society that meets the needs of its members in all spheres will have balance. Collectively the people will prosper, and individually there will be no artificially imposed hindrances to their development. So, the most significant point for the development of a healthy human society is that its focus be the development of all of its members, in all spheres. This is the foundation upon which a healthy socioeconomic structure must be based.

To develop a society which can give human beings what they

need in all spheres requires two things. First, there must be a universal outlook that does not discriminate by race, social class, cultural background, or other divisive sentiment. There must be a universal outlook which sees all living beings—not only human beings but all living beings—as expressions of the Infinite. This universal outlook will foster reverence for all life, for all beings, and it can become a solid foundation upon which to base the primary goal of the society. So, to achieve the welfare of all in the society, there must first be a universal outlook.

Second, there must be respect for the differences between people, that is to say, an acknowledgment of the diversity of human experience without judgment or the tendency to set one group against another.

If there is both a universal outlook and a respect for the uniqueness of different types of people, then there becomes a basis for a socio-economic approach which can promote the physical, psychological, and spiritual benefit of all.

## Harm to the Exploited and to the Exploiters

If the society does not meet the needs of its members, if it is solely for the benefit of an elite few whose welfare is privileged by a social and economic structure that imposes scarcity upon many to maintain the wealth of the few, then there will be imbalance in the society. A human society that lacks equity is bound to become imbalanced over time. Those who are oppressed will not be able to realize their full potential over time they will drag the society down. And those who live in the lap of luxury at the expense of others will themselves suffer due to the decadency and moral decay which they experience. Engaging in exploitation does not sit well for one who would learn to love themself. If they feel their position is gained at the expense of others, they will not feel good about themselves and, ultimately, they will also suffer.

When inequity and imbalance come to the society, suffering is pervasive. Psychologically and spiritually, all suffer. Though some may have much material luxury, they still pay a price. And those who are exploited to provide luxury to the few, they pay a different price. Their price is in the lack of adequate physical necessities or educational opportunities.

All people suffer when access to basic necessities and opportunities becomes based on sex, on race, or on cultural background. These differences become excuses for maintaining these types of inequities, and over time they cause great harm all around.

## Lack of Proper Foundations

A society may better the lives of its members, or it may impede their development. A society based in capitalistic greed, where the primary goal is to allow for the expansion of individuals to the exclusion of the needs of others, a society which emphasizes this type of socioeconomic goal will encourage greed and exploitation rather than the welfare of the collective body. It emphasizes individual initiative and development rather than collective functions.

This may work well for those individuals who can climb to the top. But since there are no controls or limits placed upon the acquisitions of individuals, some will climb over others. Over time this approach is bound to lead to an imbalanced society where there are those who have a great deal and those who have very little and are exploited by those who climb over them to gain power and riches.

If we analyze what is wrong in this approach, we see that the cornerstones or foundations necessary for the development of a healthy human society are not in place. They are not the driving force which propels social and economic growth and development. Instead, the driving force in a capitalistic system becomes individual gain and development—the right to personal acquisition rather than the development of all people in all spheres.

Over time the capitalistic system is bound to produce inequities and suppress the needs and potentials of large portions of the society. Though many may have their physical needs met, the type of materialism which accompanies capitalistic expansion leads to the suppression of psychological and spiritual needs. So, those people who have materially benefited from materialism may suffer in other spheres, and the inequities which are the result of flagrant aggressiveness in the economic sphere come to oppress all.

## Foundation of Love and Universalism

In a communist approach, there is the development of social awareness, and the welfare of the collective is considered. But there is an inherent flaw, which is that little incentive is given for individual achievement and personal advancement. The collective is given so much emphasis that the fundamental desires of a human being for their own hearth and home, for an avenue of personal advancement, these basic desires become suppressed and—like in capitalism—the goal of physical, mental, and spiritual advancement for all becomes lost. So much emphasis is placed upon collective needs that individual needs go unmet and, as in capitalism, inequity and discontent is produced.

Human beings must have opportunities for personal advancement in all spheres. Society cannot suppress spiritual exploration otherwise harm is done to all. So, communism is not the solution to the ills of capitalism. Only a society based in love and universalism, with a high regard for cardinal human values and which has as its goal the upliftment in all spheres of all of its members may succeed. Only such a society can build and establish balance.

There is great need for a new system, a new approach, both in the social and the economic spheres—one which places its emphasis upon the collective body but recognizes the needs of the individual and allows scope for the expression of those needs. That is why the Progressive Utilization Theory (PROUT) says that there should be maximum utilization of all of the potentialities and capacities of the members of society. None should be neglected; all must be given scope for full development.

This means that the expressions of mind cannot be suppressed, and that the natural human longing to strive for excellence and to achieve reward in that striving cannot be suppressed. Nor can the natural human desire for one's own home and own possessions be suppressed.

At the same time, these desires for individual development cannot be allowed to become so excessive that no consideration is given to the collective. In PROUT, emphasis is placed on the development of individual excellence and reward for the expression of that excellence, for the utilization of that skill and capacity in all spheres. But, at the same time, there is the regulation of human activity when it goes against collective welfare. So there will be a collective psychology in which collective welfare is valued. In this way, human expression may go completely unhampered and fully rewarded so long as it has no negative impact upon the society's collective development in either the social or economic spheres.

In order to achieve this balance in the economic sphere, PROUT recommends a locally based economy. This is because when the production and the consumption of goods are locally based an autonomy develops in which the people develop control over their lives. In this way, scope for exploitation is minimized.

When economic development is locally centered, those living in the region benefit the most.

With this system, those who are working in a given area must answer to their consumers. In this way they become responsible to friends and family for the work that is done and the goods produced, and at the same time they have control over what is done on the local level. This provides them opportunity for the expression of their cultural heritage and their indigenous values within the larger context of a global social order.

## Metacorporations

When economic development becomes large scale and the control of the economy is placed in the hands of metacorporations, then the welfare of the local people becomes unimportant, and these local people lose control over their lives. The conditions of their lives are dictated by the whims of some metacorporation which is completely uninvolved with them and has no reason to care for their welfare. Under such conditions the benefits of the services and the profits will not go back to the region from which they have come. Instead, the profits go into the hands of the metacorporations.

Metacorporations are those corporations which have become so vast that they have swallowed many local businesses, many local concerns, and have become worldwide in their investment and their development. Their purpose may be very narrow—that is, to make profit for themselves—but their capacity to affect the lives and welfare of people in many parts of the world becomes great. They are very large and overgrown, having allegiance to no one but themselves.

This type of large economic structure leads to economic oppression. It leads to the community's loss of control of its resources or of its ability to distribute those resources within the community. It also leads to economic oppression of different regions in the world and of different groups of people. Due to the lack of involvement with the needs of a given people in a given area, the metacorporations may become quite heartless, and there may be great hardship endured by certain people or regions.

Their goal is not the physical, mental, and spiritual development of all of the members of the society; their goal is the advancement of their profits. In this way, the economic entity becomes the god, and all of the workers' labors go to ensure its welfare and the maintenance of its status. The people themselves become the slaves of this economic god to whom they must bow down in obedience, and from whom they receive only small scraps for their cooperation. Should they refuse to cooperate with what this meta-entity desires, it may be harsh indeed with them, with no ill consequence to itself.

This economic system dominated by the global corporations is the worst type of exploitation of human beings. These meta-entities of global economic development become economic conquerors and despots to which large portions of humanity become enslaved. This is no economic system at all; it is despotic rule. This is the worst form of social development.

To develop a proper human society there must be the maintenance of local economic control so that those people who produce the goods have power over their own lives. With local economic control, they do not become the slaves of the metacorporations; they maintain power over their own communities and over their own futures. PROUT takes the approach of local economic development.

## World Government

At the same time, PROUT emphasizes the implementation of universality in the social sphere through the development of a world government. Without a global authority, the regional governments are bound to bicker and quarrel with each other over what belongs to whom, who has the better culture or system, which may lead them to have conflict with one another.

War is the worst stain upon the human society. In a balanced society all efforts must be made to see that war is ended forever and that the society lives in relative harmony.

For this there must be the adoption of universalism and the goal of collective welfare. This must be implemented in a global fashion so that the different regions, though they may have a big say in their own economic growth and development, will have to answer to a global body regarding their policies with one another. In this way, one group may not exploit another, and no nation will be allowed to go to war. They must find ways of working with one another, ways of adjusting to each other.

In this regard the global body will be a peacekeeping force and will encourage the development of universalism in outlook and respect for the differences among human beings. It will also set limits upon expansion, so that when expansion—in the individual realm and in the regional realm—becomes harmful to the collective body there will be regulation of that expansion.

In PROUT there is encouragement for personal excellence and for collective excellence, but there is not scope for exploitation. The primary goal of the society is the physical, mental and spiritual development of all its members. This is where the adaptation of a universal philosophy is essential, a philosophy that is based upon a common reverence for the interconnectedness of all living beings and for the life in every being.

# 4

# End of the Capitalist Age

Throughout history through different rites and rituals and practices, people have sought to know the Divine Entity. And in many cultures the relationship between that Entity and the individual was of primary importance. But in today's world, in most countries, that relationship is considered of little importance. There are of course those religious individuals who consider it important. But, in the main, if you go to the media of the culture you will find only nominal lip service to that spiritual relationship. You will find instead that the Divine Entity has been replaced with a god of material gain. Happiness and success in life are sought through material gain. This sentiment is dominant, and those who seek a personal relationship with the Great are ever grappling with materialist cultural norms.

Their battle with the dominant societal values is not simply outside of themselves, but inside as well. Their inner battle is between the part of them that wants to place more emphasis on a materially comfortable life and the part that wants to place emphasis on spiritual life. Meanwhile, the social fabric of the society has been eaten away as if being attacked by a cancer. The social fabric, the extended family, the nuclear family—all of the important emotional relationships and support systems—have broken down.

People feel the need to focus on earning a good income to acquire all those things they think are necessary to be happy; they have to put all of their time into this. This leads people to live in fear: what if they become a problem—an old person, a sick person, a person who cannot win the game of material gain?

Where in this arrangement is the development of the capacity to operate collectively? The collective becomes secondary to the individual and to personal gain. Where have these values come from that fail to foster the cohesion of society? Have they not come from materialism? When there is emphasis on the individual, then there will of necessity come to be a dependence on material acquisition. Even though you are alone, if you have more, you will be doing better. Or so goes the dominant social value that gives importance to acquisition of wealth.

The very fabric of the society has broken down, and the value of human relationships has become secondary. The value of family, the value of friendships, the value of community—they are secondary. As a result, when breakdowns occur and crises arise, people are left in a lonely place. Not only are they in a lonely place, they are in a very vulnerable position if they are unable to make the grade as a good earner. Get sick and they might be without care. Get old and they might have to go to a nursing home.

Not only has the relationship to the Divine Entity broken down but valuing others has also broken down—the value of family, clan, and community has broken down. Even the nuclear family isn't healthy: so many marriage breakups, so many single families.

The society has lost its balance. It has come out of balance because the dominant capitalist mentality has become disruptive to fundamental human needs. Human beings need to have clan and family, need to love each other, need to depend on each other, in interdependent, interwoven relationships. That is the strength of the human society.

Materialism has grown to a point where it is a cancer in the society. It is a cancer in Western societies and now in Eastern societies as well, for they have adopted it in a hungry way. In their hunger they are adopting everything, swallowing it. And they will swallow the disease as well. One can no longer say that materialism is strictly a feature of Western culture. Around the world materialism grows as a cancer in society.

## The Disgruntled Intellectuals

The next age after the capitalist age is the warrior age. It comes about through the workers revolution. And what is the workers revolution? It is when the classes that have been exploited in the capitalist age rebel against capitalist dominance in a forceful way to break the capitalist grip on social dominance.

Who is it that feels most suppressed? It is the intellectuals who are highly disgruntled by their situation, who feel suppressed. Many of these disgruntled intellectuals are of a religious mind. Where is the largest group of these disgruntled intellectuals in the world today? They are in the Middle East. And there is another large group of these religious individuals in America—the religious fundamentalists who are threatened by the materialism and secularism of the capitalist era. They are also among the religious fundamentalists in India.

They are suppressed intellectuals. Their minds are dominated by religious thinking, and they do not like materialism. They feel their authority is suppressed. They feel that their true values, the true ways of their religion, have been suppressed by the materialism of the West. They are the largest group to feel disgruntled with materialism.

## The Way Forward

There are also many intelligent people who realize the predicament of the society but who do not want to go back to the past, to the times when the religious institutions dominated the society. They want to march forward to a new future having a new spirituality. Both groups—the religious fundamentalists and the forward-thinking intellectuals—have a commonality. Both are disgruntled and feeling suppressed; both are coming to want the overthrow of the capitalist age. But their idea of what to do is very different; one is dogma-based, the other spiritual-based.

Time does not march backwards; the past cannot be recreated. The inevitable call of spirit to that deep personal connection within, that will now rise. Those who look forward, who would embrace new values based on a spirituality unencumbered by dogma, they are the harbingers of a new age.

An idea whose time has come is the most powerful weapon in the world, and they have ideas whose time has come. It is time for them to put those ideas forward. There are today millions of people who are now turning to meditation, wanting to develop a personal relationship with the Supreme. Many of them realize that a good job and lots of money aren't really making them happy. They want something more. In this realization, many seek an intimate relationship with the Great.

The feelings of stress and strain, depression and anxiety, are on a mass scale as never before. Why? Because the society has lost balance. Naturally people are suffering under these circumstances.

They may have full bellies, and they may live in big homes, but their basic human needs are not being met. Their relationship to the Divine and their relationships to each other are disrupted by the disease stemming from materialism.

People cannot be kept penned forever. The restlessness within, the realization, "I am not happy," comes to them. And so they search. By droves they are turning to spiritual life. Around the globe it is happening. The movement needs no leader, needs no organization. It is the spontaneous response to the imbalanced condition of human society. The yearning to find the way out of darkness is inherent in the human heart.

In today's world there is a growing clash between the disgruntled intellectuals and the capitalists. This clash will only intensify. There is to be found among the disgruntled intellectuals both the dogma-based and the spiritual-based ideologies. It may appear at present that the dogma-based forces are more dominant than spiritual-based because the spirit based is like a wave rising from the depths. It has no leader; it has no organization. It is grounded in a personal, individual experience. It has no history, yet its roots are ancient. It is a wave rising in the society, and as this wave rises, the desire to change the society in a positive way will grow in magnitude.

An idea whose time has come can be a greater force than any weapon. It will change the world.

# 5

# Managing the Fall of Capitalism

In capitalism the theory is that entrepreneurs, desiring their own profit and competing with each other, will be inspired to higher quality work so that superior goods and services will flourish. This system originated as an advance in medieval village economies. In a village economy, there may originally have been only one cobbler, but then another cobbler opens a shop. Now there are two cobblers, and they are in competition. When there was only one cobbler, there was no competition. He could do poor work, and the people would have to settle for shoes of poor craftsmanship. But when the second cobbler set up shop the two cobblers competed with each other, and the villagers could go to the new one who does the better quality of work. Then, the original cobbler will have an incentive to improve the quality of his craft. Through such competition, this early form of capitalism was very effective at bringing a better quality of products to the people.

From these origins, the capitalist system has grown until now there are international corporations of immense size and owning many subsidiary corporations. They have become so vast in their scope that they begin to resemble the single cobbler in the village economy of old. Their goal is to eliminate the competition, to eliminate anything that would stand in the way of their profits. They have come to this approach by the same system that inspired the village cobblers into competition and that promoted superior quality work. But now, there is no village; there is the reach of the international corporations across the globe. They own many subsidiary companies, and they have become very powerful entities. But these entities have one purpose still: to out compete all others so as to increase their profits and their wealth.

They have now become so powerful that their capacity to increase profit and wealth lies primarily in their ability to suppress competition—and even to influence governments—to get the most they can. The original system of healthy competition has been corrupted, and the powerful corporations' intention to gain profit is now so extreme that they control great amounts of wealth, and they have now become the dominant controllers of power in the world.

It is mainly the greed of the multinational corporations that have brought the world to the brink of catastrophe. These corporations want only to increase their profits. The goal of improved quality of work, driven by healthy competition, that was seen in the village economy has waned. The motivation is less to improve quality as a means to increase profit; it is to control the market, control the buyers, control the workers. The capitalist economy now gives expression to extreme greed.

## Power Over Governments

Those who live by the sword, die by the sword. The sword that the great corporate entities live by is that of cutting through all obstacles to attain the maximum profit. That has meant the acquisition and use of power to control governments so that the governments do not stand in their way and benefit them in so many ways.

Due to this, governments have become weak. The corporations are sufficiently powerful to exert their influence over governmental bodies. The regulatory systems and the laws that are intended to control the excesses and harm of the corporate entities are weakened or ignored, leaving them free to pursue their profits and to acquire more power. The goal is no longer to increase product quality so as to increase profit, but to increase power in the world—and not for the benefit of the society, but for greater corporate gain. They exert all manner of power and control to gain the proper environment for maximizing their bottom line.

So, the competition that was a healthy approach in the simple medieval village economy has now become detrimental to the society. The goal of capitalism at this point is less about quality and improvement in services and more about acquiring power and profit. With their ability to influence governmental bodies, regulation is stifled, and the powerful multinational corporations are able to increase their influence and their profit relatively unchecked.

One result of this unchecked greed was the 2008 mortgage crisis, centered in America. Federal government regulation and oversight of the banks was weakened, creating an opportunity for banks to maximize their profit by pushing alluring mortgages. The banks and mortgage brokers then encouraged people to overextend their debt. This generated even greater profits for the banks. But their reckless pursuit of profits was done without care for the welfare of the people acquiring the mortgages.

With the lax regulations, the corporate lenders saw great

opportunity to maximize profit, and their greed drove them to acquire more and more profit even when real money was not there. Trading in the lending market became increasingly insubstantial and theoretical. This caused a great imbalance. So long as profit was being made, the practicality of having real money behind the loans, and the consideration of the impacts on the ordinary person, became irrelevant. It was inevitable that this would all come to a tragic end.

## Enlightened Socialism

The world stands at a critical juncture, and over the next few years the situation will become more critical. The world will have to make a choice: Will governments regain their strength? And will they recognize that they exist in an international community that requires global regulation? The world today is like the Wild West run by the fastest gun—that is, run by the multinational corporations. There is no government of the world, so the multinational corporations, with their drive for acquisition and profit, like the Old West outlaws, have taken over. It is time that the governments unite and face the crisis caused by their failure to take responsibility for economic regulation.

Beyond the global economic problems are a stack of other critical problems that are also coming to fruition. There is oil depletion, climate change, environmental pollution, excessive population, natural disasters, food shortages, water pollution, water shortages, etc. These are all coming along with the economic crisis, and their mutual interaction will magnify the impacts of global crises, should proper actions not be taken. The world is coming to a place of crisis—again, because there is no governmental body, no multinational body, to look to the welfare of all of Earth's people. There is no one to take this charge. The capitalist cowboys are running free, taking humanity to the brink. Can we continue to let them be unregulated worldwide entities?

The current situation has created an opportunity for the governments of the world to band together, to unify themselves and form a type of enlightened socialism. Under the approach of this enlightened socialism, the governments would work together to regulate greed. They would take forceful action to see that capitalist privatization and greed come under the control and that corporations serve the welfare of the international community, and not solely their private profits. At present, the intention of capitalism is to create profits for the corporations. If the intention were instead to include to promote the welfare of the world community, this would end the oppressive dominance of capitalism.

With a worldwide approach, governed by a world organization, power could be given back to local businesses and to local communities. There could be a uniting to promote local economies. This would create grounding in a practical economics, not a theoretical one based on monies that don't exist and on debt and more debt.

What if governments also decided to erase all foreign debts and start afresh with no national debts, no international debts. What if the playing field were leveled? The governments, again taking a worldwide approach, could decide to form one type of exchange—no dollar, no Euro; there would be one exchange and all debts of nations erased. And then ample monies could be directed to support and develop small businesses and economic diversity. Economic diversity, small business development, and local economic independence would be promoted as much as possible and directed toward meeting the basic needs of all peoples. And, as well, strict regulation would be put in place to suppress the greed of capitalism. This enlightened socialist approach would solve today's growing economic crisis.

## Critical Juncture

At this critical juncture, it may be that the global community will come together and create a rational approach that serves human welfare. But it may also be that capitalist greed will remain so dominant that this does not happen. In the present crisis there are two possible directions that may be taken. One is some type of enlightened socialism. The other is totalitarian control by those who are motivated to run the world to serve their greed. Should this later approach dominate, it will not last long. Their exploitation and greed, without consideration of the needs of people, will bring their downfall. But in the course of this downfall there would be much suffering.

The world stands at a turning point, at a juncture. It may be that capitalism will give way to a type of enlightened socialism to pull the world out of this crisis. But it may also be that the multinational corporate powers attain more dominance and even further utilize the weakened governments under their control and establish a short reign of capitalist tyranny.

## Change of Eras

The early capitalist system that was originally built in which the village craftsmen and merchants competed to produce higher quality goods brought social progress. The early merchant society was a healthy advance. But, as with all class dominance, when the capitalist era reaches towards the end, it becomes so extreme that it becomes a force against the human society.

Having reached this extreme, change is inevitable. There will be mass revolution, led by those enlightened intellectuals who care for the welfare of humanity. The people cannot lead themselves as a mass, so the aware intellectuals must give the leadership to bring forward change.

What follows the mass revolution? Then the warrior class will come to the fore and take the lead. A warrior society is not necessarily a martial society. In a warrior society, it is warrior values that determine the approach of the society. In the capitalist society, the value is on personal gain; greed is the motive. In the warrior society, the dominant values are duty and honor. Warriors live for duty and honor. The warrior society is not a military society, but it is a very well-ordered society, as people uphold their social duty, and maintain their collective responsibility. There is not the individualistic indulgence of capitalist society, but a strong sense of duty to collective interests. The growing reaction to capitalism's neglect of individuals, communities, and the environment—and all the insecurity and suffering this has caused—will naturally give momentum to the rise of the warrior society.

The wheels of social evolution now turn, and that system of competition that once created increased well-being and wealth has become a tyranny upon the people—oppressing them with materialism, oppressing them with the power of the profit-driven corporate entities. They have lived by their greed, and so they are falling. They may rally for yet a few more years of dominance, but still they will fall. So, it is now a time of change.

These are times of dynamic change and of great opportunity for humanity. But naturally, in times of great change, of a shifting of class dominance, change is not easy. How deep and how difficult it becomes will depend upon the response of the world's peoples, and upon the availability of a guiding ideology that can provide enlightened solutions.

6

# Transition to a Regulated Global Society

What we now experience under capitalism is economic greed of extreme proportions. At the inception of the capitalist era, the capitalist system was a healthy development. Each merchant competed with others for consumers' patronage by increasing the quality of their goods, and this competition worked to increase quality and service. It was a healthy system in the early days of the rise of the merchant class. But it is the natural flow of the social cycle (see Appendix 1) that every class that comes to dominance eventually deteriorates. It develops to the point where it can no longer sustain itself and it topples, or is toppled, from power.

In the case of the end of the capitalist class, people will rise *en masse* against the domination of the wealthy merchants. There will be a revolution by those who become sufficiently disgruntled as to resist or to build out alternatives to capitalist dominance.

There has been a transition to a global society in which the corporate conglomerates of the grand capitalists have become multinational in scope, with subsidiaries throughout the world and having hundreds of corporations under one conglomerate banner. They have become so powerful that they can exercise great influence over governments, so that even the power and authority of national governments are weakening.

These global corporate entities are also able to exert great influence over the economies of different countries, playing one against the other to best get their profit-driven needs met. If they can get their cheap labor in India or China, and sell their products to the United States, they will do so. They operate internationally, and they are not concerned with the welfare of anyone but themselves and with their bottom line. They do not plan for global development. They simply plan based on their own greed.

Due to their power and control, the multinational conglomerates have been able to influence many countries' policies. They come and take the cheap labor, and they lobby for deregulation so they can operate as they wish. They have changed laws and regulations to maximize their profits. Their goal is always profit. And because they have overextended their greed, they have slit their own throats with their own swords because they have weakened their markets, destabilized the world, and have brought the world to a point of crisis. Capitalism will fall, as those that live by the sword die by the sword. They live by their greed; they will die by their greed.

Some may compare the present situation to the Great Depression of the 1930s, which was the first major sign of the deterioration of capitalism. However, global capitalism was not then developed as it is today; the economy of one country did not so affect the economy of other countries. In today's world of global corporations, having many subsidiaries in many countries, there is a global economy. But there is no humanistic and thoughtful global entity to make decisions. Rather, decisions are made by this corporation or that, each trying to maximize profits.

So, when they put their factories in India, Philippines, or China and then sell their products in Europe or America, they are not thinking, "What will be the impact on the world?" They are simply thinking, "How much money can I make?" When they determine prices and manipulate markets, they are not thinking, "What will be the long-term repercussions for the affected societies?" Due to their shortsightedness and greed, they have created a very precarious situation.

## Need for Global Leadership

There is a deeper underlying cause for the current situation. It is that globalism—the movement towards a global, one-world society—is without any governing body. There is no global body responsible for governance over these greedy corporate cowboys and for seeing to the welfare of the people of the world.

Without the leadership and policies to govern the global situation, the multinational corporations have followed their own capitalist instincts and made a mess. They are not out to harm anyone; they are simply following their nature as capitalist merchants. However, they have grown so large and so powerful that they are destructive even to themselves. The economies of countries have become destabilized due to deregulation and economic meddling by multinational corporations and, at a deeper level, due to the lack of a global governing body representing the needs of the people of the world.

The solution to today's crises is, first and foremost, to form a global body that can reckon with global economic problems, as well as with global political and ecological problems. This body can oversee the distribution of resources, based on the motive of promoting the welfare of all people. It can implement economic solutions that are cross-cultural and multinational.

Nationalism does not work in today's world, and it is reaching its end. National autonomy assumes that a nation can exist separately from others and simply pursue its own welfare. But those days are gone. Today's political leaders know it, and they are trying to adjust. They work for their separate countries but know that they cannot solve their problems independently of others. Each country tries to cling to its autonomy, yet their cooperation increases out of necessity. The necessity in today's world is for collaborative summits and establishing a governing body that can regulate and coordinate the world economic situation and that can prevent wars.

## Following the Example of the European Union

The economic activities of one nation affects the economic activities of all nations, and the United States economy in particular affects all nations. The Americans cannot solve their problems without the cooperation of others, and others cannot solve their problems when the Americans are in trouble. So, everyone is in trouble. Individually they cannot solve their problems and they recognize this. There is too much inherent interdependence within economic markets. The problems are international, and so the solution-makers must be international. This is a known reality in the political world of today. But what is said differs from what is needed, for there is a clinging to the autonomy of nations.

The nations of the world need to be in a coordinated whole, much as the countries of Europe have come into the European Union. The world must come into some type of union for peace, ecological protection, and for economic coordination. Has the European Union helped Europe in general? Has the softening of the national boundaries so that the Europeans can go here and there helped Europe? Definitely. Europe is thriving, relatively speaking.

A global body should be created, and it should set up an economic council to coordinate global economic development. This global economic council should develop a true global economy, responsibly managed, with goals for global economic development, coordination and distribution of resources—development that is not based on corporate greed but based on human needs as perceived by a responsible international council representing all countries. In this properly managed global economy, the corporate entities would operate under firm regulation by the global economic council.

## Transition to a New Era

A shift away from the age of capitalists is inevitable. This shift will get advanced through the workers revolution. Who is it that will undertake the workers revolution? It is the disgruntled people who want change. They are intelligent people who are tired of the illogic and inhumanity of the current situation and want an improvement. Through their mass demands will come change. It will come from the bottom up, from the populace spurred and led by the ideas of the disgruntled and alternative thinking people in the society.

These intelligent people see that the present system is not working and are beginning to demand something else. Their ideas are catching on and becoming popular. The masses of the society want change to occur. Many are beginning to side with the alternative-thinking people and to realize, "These corporations are leading us down a false road of economic hope. We're just getting used by them."

The ideas of progressive thinking, intelligent people are becoming more accepted. This kind of thinking en masse will increasingly come into prominence. There is a change that is gaining momentum—a shift from capitalist dominance to the workers revolution led by the disgruntled and alternative thinking members of the society.

To sustain the revolutionary change after the workers revolution, there will be need for more discipline and regulation in the society. This will bring a shift to a society dominated by the values of duty, discipline, and morality. It will be a well-regulated society in which no one can greedily amass profits. The regulatory discipline of the society will increase. People's sense of duty to the welfare of humanity will become dominant. It will no longer be acceptable to engage in economic development at the expense of others. This will be a society which places duty, discipline and morality over money. It will be a society of good quality.

All societies have had merchants, and there will still be merchants. There will still be corporations; there will still be a vital economy. In all societies, there must be economic enterprise, money, and trade. All of these functions will go on, but the values of the society will shift. The glory will not be in becoming an economic entrepreneur that amasses wealth. What will be of value is the noble person who is dutiful and follows moral social action. That will be seen as the indicator of personal success.

## Emergence of a Well-Regulated Global Economy

Out of necessity, people will begin to build a strong global political body that can implement strong global economic solutions—solutions that arrange for the rational distribution of resources and that strictly regulate the multinational corporate entities. There needs to be a regulatory body that guides these decisions in a cooperative way between nations so that there can be a coordinated policy that benefits everyone.

Naturally, some nations will be richer than others. The world regulatory body cannot produce complete equality. Equality is not the goal; welfare is the goal. Some parts of the world are more developed; some parts are less developed. Each nation will grow at their own rate, even in a world society. Distribution of resources will not be the same everywhere; but if the principles of PROUT are implemented, the basic necessities will be provided for all in a humanitarian way.

What is at stake is the survival of humanity in the face of pollution, over population, ecological destruction, economic collapse, climate change, and natural disasters. If all of this is to be faced, it cannot occur under the dominating influence of corporate power and corporate greed. Global crises must be managed by a responsible global council that addresses human needs. Who will address the crisis of massive natural disasters or global pandemics? How can the economies of countries be coordinated so that everyone can be living in security and welfare? How can the world protect itself from nuclear proliferation? How can the food supply be maintained to feed the growing population? These are critical questions that, along with others, must be addressed and answered.

Necessity demands that these issues be properly solved. For this, there must be dutiful, ethical and intelligent people who come into power in a global society, rather than the big corporations being the dominant power. Because of necessity, we will be seeing the end of capitalism, the end of the capitalist era, and the transition to a well-disciplined and regulated global society in which the dominant objective is human welfare.

# 7

# A Time to Be Dynamically Active

There is a shift taking place in the world, and it is going in two directions. On the one hand, the world is dealing with great imbalances. Human population is too high, causing excessive loss of habitat and depletion of natural resources. Individual greed is the dominant motivation in society. Economic dynamics are imbalanced. And there is a vying for world dominance by nations and by the economic fiefdoms of the multinational corporations.

On the other hand, there is the growth of the Internet with its great capacity for bringing the world into one mind and interweaving human awareness. Then there is a great spiritual awakening, so that meditation is becoming commonplace. And there is a growing awareness of the need for environmental restoration on a global scale.

These positive movements are going on while at the same time the population is growing out of control, species are dying, pollution is poisoning the air and water, natural resources are being depleted, food supply is in jeopardy, wars are occurring, and the economy is unstable. All of this is making the global situation critical.

A gangly state of confusion and awkward growth exists in the human society at this time—much like the puberty of a child. But, as we know, the teenage child will continue to grow, and they will mature into a young man or young woman. The awkwardness, the confusion, is a stage of development, a stage of evolution. This is also a stage in the evolution of the earth itself, of Gaia.

Human beings are the children, the very life forms, of Gaia. Our bodies are made of this earth; our psyches are connected to this earth. We are her evolution. She is evolving and her evolution is one. What is occurring is the evolution of the earth. Our bodies are made of Gaia.

Gaia is evolving. As it evolves greater manifestation of consciousness, some things which were cannot continue, while some things which will be are not yet established. This is the nature of planetary evolution at present. The ways which will be do not yet exist. They may exist in small formations, in certain ways, but in the overall society the situation is still awkward and lacking balance. We see the reflection of this imbalance expressed in the breakdown of families and of communities. It is also to be seen in the rampant depression and anxiety among people because of the lack of community and the lack of security in their lives. It is a sociological ailment affecting individuals psychologically, and it affects much of society. A sickness is there. It can be seen in the psyches of many people, but these psychic symptoms are ailments of the society that cause people to suffer.

The times demand our maturation and adjustment. It is time for progressive ideas to come forward and for people to unite together. Naturally, the reactionary forces which pull humanity back towards the more limited approach, the more individualistic greed-oriented approach, feel very threatened because they sense their day has come. This is the end of the capitalist era. There is a transition of consciousness occurring, and with it comes the end of an age.

## Need for Solution-Based Understandings

In these times it is becoming easier to bring forward ideas which are transformative. The ideas that represent the past—the ideas of greed-based capitalism—are becoming harder and harder to sustain. But the strength of the emerging progressive awareness, and of the unity of people around this awareness, is growing strong. The very existence of these transformative ideas is the expression of the freeing of consciousness and the dwindling down on what was.

In the present situation there is great need for solution-based understandings. How can the world be made to work? Where can the resources come from? If the amount of money spent in wars were put into the development of sustainable resources, what would happen? Even though questions such as these seem theoretical, they should be explored. Workable solutions come out of clear visioning.

As the grip of the past gives way there will be a shift, there will be change. But the capitalist era will not give way without resistance. The big capitalists do not just say, "Oh, you want to take over? We'll just fade away." There must be a struggle for change. There is now opportunity for the new to arise, but this is occurring within the struggle for the birth of a new form and an ending and relinquishing of the old. There is always struggle in this process.

The forces of evolution are with those that want change. So, they will feel that energetically they are supported, and that feeling will grow within them. "I can do this. I can make progress. I can make change." This feeling will emerge and strengthen within them.

The forces of evolution are supporting change, but through our efforts we must do the work. In times past, working for evolutionary change was like climbing a steep mountain. It was hard to move, and much of our struggle came to naught. Now, increasingly, it is more like climbing a gentle grade, and many of our efforts bear fruit. But still someone must do it. All social evolution is built on the work of people.

There are people who in their fear and ignorance do harm to the general good but are too fearful to see it. Many of these people, if educated, if befriended, will put their resources toward positive change. If they are shown a better way that works, they will follow it. They are practical people who are not going to follow those who only condemn and criticize everything but are without good solutions. If they are offered good solutions, if they are inspired, they will turn around.

This may even happen with some heads of multinational corporations. Many of them are good people who have never been shown a better way. Of course, there are also those who have malevolent intentions. But many are just following what they know to work and what they have been taught.

## From Criticism to Solutions

There is a kind of negativity in some activist circles; there are those who criticize and bemoan the state of the world. But as social change moves forward, it will grow beyond the people who are stuck in negativity to the people who are positive and action-oriented. It may even come to include people in large businesses who have lost their faith in that system and seek a new paradigm. They are action-oriented, they may recognize that society needs a new direction, but unless they can be given viable solutions, they will not join progressive causes. They are dynamic people with great capacities to effect change. If they are given positive and inspiring solutions, they may be drawn like the moth to the flame. The tendency to criticize, criticize is a natural reaction to the feeling of disempowerment in the face of great problems that people felt they could not solve. But the situation is changing. It is time to put aside this negative approach and take an approach of feeling empowerment to provide practical solutions and affect fundamental change.

There is a great swell of awareness, and it will only grow in magnitude. But there are many who are restless. They see the problems; they see the difficulties; they see the collision course ahead. But they don't know what to do. They need solution-based ideas. The more solution-based ideas there are, the more these ideas can be implemented, and then the less severe, the less devastating, will be the process of change. The degree to which positive solutions can be implemented is the degree to which the present evolutionary shift will happen more gently. Humanity is being drawn toward a new era. It is a time to be dynamically active.

8

# Liberation from the Oppression of Materialism

For a great many in the world today, oppression arises from the false ideology of materialism. They become oppressed by the dogma of consumption, believing that if material acquisition or consumption will make them happy. Is this not an oppression? Materialism oppresses the human spirit. It makes people feel disheartened, depressed, disassociated from the power of their spirit.

People are socialized to buy and consume. In this way, they assume the identity of a consumer. But what depth of the heart is fulfilled in consumption? Consumers become like hungry ghosts. Their connection with community is broken; their extended families broken. More and more, even their nuclear families are broken. They become lonely. An emptiness develops in the heart, a hollowness, and this oppression diminishes their human spirit. Consumerism cannot satisfy the human heart. It is a false ideology.

Materialism is a great affliction that oppresses millions of people. It's been an affliction of the West that has now spread to the East. It oppresses virtually the entire planet, and the large corporations want to keep people in this state of oppression.

## Rallying the Human Spirit Through Spirituality

But emerging beneath the wave of materialism there is a rallying of the human spirit to new ways of thinking. Spirituality, in particular, has direct relevance to ending the oppression of materialism, because the spirituality of today lies not only in achieving personal realization but also in answering the call to action in the human society. There is in this spirituality both the path to divinity and the call to see to the care and love for all beings.

When human beings are treated with disrespect, when they are oppressed, exploited and humiliated—all for the benefit of others—it is an offense to spirit, for each and every living being is a manifestation divinity. All living beings are a part of that Great Entity. None should be treated harmfully. This harming of living beings causes psychic imbalances in the world.

It is natural for human beings to love each other, to love other creatures, to want to be close, to want to be connected. In that connection the boundaries of "I" and "mine" are crossed, and one feels the completeness of their spirit. When one laughs in spontaneous joy with one's friends and loved ones, one feels the connection of spirit; one experiences the union in which the sense of separateness is lost. When one goes into deep meditation, one experiences the feeling of that union. Then coming back into the world that feeling can be brought into the life. No one is an island to live their life alone without the community of their fellow beings. All living beings are a part of a whole. Together they share this world.

## Restoring Balance

When so many human beings suffer unwanted pains and sorrows and are exploited for the greed of others, this creates an imbalance in the world. Balance is destroyed and disharmony comes in the society. As the society becomes more entrenched in disharmony, it destroys the wholeness of the community. Many things of value fall away. The fabric of the society is destroyed, leaving people with much pain and suffering and unmet needs. In this state, meeting the genuine needs of human beings is not what drives the values of society. What drives the society is the ideology of materialism, of greed and consumerism—propagated so that the few can become very wealthy at the expense of the many.

But the awareness that materialism is not working is growing. In the West, the ideology of materialism has been around longer, and the true poison of it has been ingested. In the East it is still popular because it is new and fascinating, and so the hidden poison of it has not been as fully felt. In the West, people are sick with the poison. The poison has destroyed communities, it has destroyed families, and people find themselves lonely, displaced, unhappy, restless. They are beginning to see what they do not have, and this ideology of materialism and consumerism is losing status.

In the West, it can now be seen that capitalism is becoming less popular; its disfavor is growing as people feel the sting of what they have lost. In the East, the sting is not fully felt; but it will come there too.

People are feeling the sting and realizing that they have lost something very precious. They increasingly want to gather to find connection and build community. The movement that is developing to build in this way is as yet a small expression of what will be. As times get harder, it will only grow.

This is what lies in humanity's future, because this movement expresses a fundamental urge to restore balance in the society. The pendulum that has swung to one end, impelled by an ideology that breeds great imbalances, will now swing the other way. There will be much receptivity to this movement, and that receptivity will only grow.

PROUT's concepts will be warmly received—especially in the West where the people feel such psychic pain. People want to come together, to feel nurtured and cared for, to see that human beings are treated well and fairly. Not only human beings, but all living beings.

It is an opportune time to bring forward this ideology to replace the defective materialist ideology and to heal the ills that materialism has created. Receptivity will grow and grow to the notions expressed in PROUT.

## Nuclear Revolution

According to PROUT there are three forms of revolution. One is *palatial revolution*, which occurs when there is a change of regime but with no substantive change of the institutions or the guiding ideology. There may be new leadership, but it will not change the oppression people feel, for the oppressive ideology remains in place, the lifestyle remains in place, so the fundamental problems will still exist.

A second type of revolution is *pyramidical revolution*. This occurs when an enlightened leadership initiates a wave of transformation in the society. It comes from enlightened leaders who are able to inspire the people to undertake deep social transformation. But is there any enlightened leadership at present to inspire the people to overthrow the oppression of materialism? No, there is not. There are leaders who may champion some progressive reforms, but they do not stand against the ideology that is at the root of society's oppression. So, pyramidical revolution cannot be looked to as a way to end the oppression.

The third type is *nuclear revolution*. In nuclear revolution there is a deep cultural and ideological shift. This shift is brought deep into the hearts of the people, and then political change comes as a result. Nuclear revolution doesn't start with political change; it evokes political change. It is because the hearts and minds of people begin to want change that they become mobilized. When the time is right, if there is hope and a vision of a way forward, then the people will rush to it.

## Liberating the Human Heart

In most of the world, people have embraced the self-centered ideology of capitalism. But now people are hurting, and they are looking for solutions to their pain. The human spirit cannot be suppressed for long; it doesn't want to be mired in materialism. One more thing to consume, to wear, to acquire, to collect—this will not satisfy the human heart. The human heart wants expansiveness. It wants to feel the experience of transcendence, whether it is in human relations, in connection to the natural world, or in deep meditation. The human heart wants to expand; it wants to feel love unconditional; it wants to know itself.

This fundamental spirit of humanity cannot be suppressed for long. Perhaps it can be dampened, but what happens when it is dampened? Depression becomes the number one illness. What is the solution? It is to unfold the human spirit in interconnectedness and wholeness.

People are beginning to seek this, and the movement in this direction is growing. It is not just be found among the disgruntled intellectuals or in alternative communities. The ailment has not fully hit in the East; they have not yet experienced the full symptoms. But in the West, people are beginning to awaken.

It is a time of great transformation. There will inevitably be struggle and hardships. But as people come closer to each other, as they connect in community, and as they feel a deeper inner connection with the Supreme Entity which binds all life together in love, great and positive things are bound to happen. The future of humanity is bright.

9

# Pathway to a Bright Future

Throughout the world, people and communities are coming to realize that the approach of economic globalism is not working. People's needs are not getting adequately met and local communities have lost control over their economies. So, many people are calling for regional economic autonomy.

PROUT also calls for regional autonomy. But the PROUT approach recognizes that regional economic autonomy cannot stand on its own, that it must occur within a well-regulated system of global coordination and that for this an international coordinating body is necessary.

Consider the situation of providing for people's most basic need, that of food. How would provision of food be assured to all under a system of decentralized economic development? Countries in dry regions—such as Bahrain, Saudi Arabia, and Libya—must import certain foods. The same is true in very cold regions. So, there needs to be trade. But in the PROUT system, rather than having corporate conglomerates making the decisions to produce here and sell there, each region would have an economy with as much autonomy as possible. These autonomous regional economies can ship their excess production out to those in need, and so trade will occur. But they retain their economic autonomy; they will not work for a multinational corporation.

It will take time to make this shift. The solutions to the immediate economic problems will inevitably move in that direction, but it will not occur automatically. For more immediate solutions, there will be a need to establish a world council to coordinate the bailout of companies and countries—a kind of coordination among the different countries on a plan for stabilization. There will need to be a plan for stabilization so that unemployment can be lessened, and people can have work and get their necessities met. To do this, governments must take over the leadership of economic affairs that have been in the hands of the multinational corporations. When governments take over this leadership, they will take the reins of the economy and be able to invest in the future of their economies. Thus, it will move toward economic socialism. This is not to say there will be no individual merchants, or even no multinational corporations (at least for a time). But the relationships will change. These solutions are necessary at this time.

## Need for International Coordinating Body

PROUT advocates the ideal of local economic autonomy. But what does that look like in a given situation? In America, in the state of California, many vegetables can be grown. But in Alaska in the winter it is difficult to produce vegetables, other than in hot houses that are very costly to operate. If the Alaskan people want to eat vegetables in winter, they will either have to import them or to pay high prices for hot house grown vegetables, in which case only the rich could afford to eat vegetables on a regular basis. California can have more autonomy, but a part of its economic autonomy will be selling its vegetables to other regions. Part of the economic autonomy of Alaska will be buying vegetables, because they cannot produce enough. Of course, to the extent that Alaskans are able to produce vegetables, they should do so.

Desert countries also cannot produce sufficient food. Nor can cold, high plateau countries, like Mongolia. So, what will people in these areas—in high plateaus and in deserts—do for food? They will have to be in economic coordination with regions in fertile areas of the world that are capable of producing greater quantities of food.

This coordination does not occur effectively in the current situation because of the irresponsible corporate cowboys who rule the global economy. They come in, they sell here and buy there, but not based on the needs of the different regions. They take control of the regions away from the people and act out of their personal capitalist mandate to earn ever more profits. They run the economy as they please, and not as is needed by the people. Of course, they fulfill people's needs in so much as they can have a good market for their goods. But their goal is not to fulfill anyone's needs; it is to make money. In their dominance they have been irresponsible, and they have botched it.

There is a growing need for an international coordinating body, and that international body will need to distribute economic power in a way that increases local economic autonomy. But they will also need to regulate the global economy very assertively. If California decides that they have lots of fruits and vegetables and much of the world does not, so that they can charge high prices for their produce because others are desperate and must buy no matter what they are charged, then what happens? Greed takes over. The international coordinating body must be able to say to California, "We are regulating your trade. You cannot charge above this amount, otherwise you are exploiting others." In this way, the international body will keep the global economy regulated.

This is where the value of a warrior society comes in. The warrior society will be very capable of strictly regulating and maintaining a well run world order. But such a society is down the road. At present, there is the chaos and struggle of the transition from one system to another.

## Necessity Will Bring Change

Naturally, in a time like this, when there is upheaval and transition, people will become frightened. They want to retreat into themselves, and so protectionism will come into place. However, necessity speaks louder than protectionism, because protectionism, just like failing capitalist values, will not meet the needs of the day.

The isms of protectionism and fundamentalism naturally arise in reaction to the uncertain and frightening nature of the times. But they will not carry the day. What will carry the day will be that which looks most likely to provide for the survival for humanity.

How can we reassure those who are in fear and are attracted to divisive *isms*? We must appeal to their logic and their need to survive. But if, in their fear, they become irrational, they will do so. Eventually, however, the irrational approaches will fade—just as already many fundamentalist approaches have arisen but are not carrying the day. And they will not carry the day because these approaches cannot meet people's need. Need is critical. If a society cannot meet people's need, the society will perish. Faced with perishing, most people will do what is necessary to save themselves. There is a strong drive in the human species to adapt and do what is needed to survive.

To survive, humanity must follow the path toward decentralized economic autonomy with global coordination. People will do what they do for necessity. If in the short run it looks like having an economic bailout will help certain corporations stay alive so that the society may struggle on a little longer, that will likely be done. Necessity pushes it. But when the realization comes that these policies aren't adequate, necessity will push for greater steps to be taken.

Necessity demands change, and people come up to the mark or they perish. It is that simple. It is not intellectual; it has nothing to do with beliefs or politics.

## Need to Change Society's Value Base

In bringing forward PROUT solutions to the growing economic problems, we should not focus on local economic autonomy on the one hand, or on establishing a global coordinating body on the other hand. We must talk about both. We must talk about how to establish economic autonomy because in the global development that economic autonomy will eventually become the prevailing mode. So that must be encouraged while also encouraging the need for a coordinated world economy having a neohumanist intent—that is, being guided by spiritual-humanist values.

The struggle that is to be fought is not with a human enemy. It is with the out-of-control mess that has been left in the wake of the dying capitalist order. In the era of capitalist dominance, everything is for personal gain. The dominant motivation of this society is to think: "How can I become economically secure and safe and have a great deal of personal wealth?" This approach, placing fundamental value on personal gain, has led to this global economic mess. So, the need to change the value base must be addressed, and it must then be explained to people what is the beneficial impact that this change of values will have.

When the dominant value base of people shifts to building community, to looking out for neighbors, to making their community sustainable, to coming back to family, then people can begin to root themselves into something solid, something simple, something stable that they can relate to. In this way, the values will shift from seeking to have more for one's self to being a part of a functional community—where there is duty to one's neighbors, duty to one's society, duty to one's family, and where the measure of a successful person is that they shoulder those duties well and improve the general welfare of all.

This is at the heart of the change from capitalist values to warrior values, and this is the shift that is now going on. However, the progressive minded people that are in the forefront of making changes, they are not warriors. Most don't want a regulated, duty-oriented society; most can't relate to this. They are rebels; they are against the established order. They may reject the capitalist values and institutions and embrace alternative ideals, but few have embraced warrior values of honoring social duty. Yet, as they settle, as they ground, as they seek to manifest their ideas in community, in connection with others, they will learn the importance of loyalty and duty, and many will embrace the warrior values.

## Giving People a Pathway to Survival

When presenting PROUTist solutions to people, to the degree that they are open, we can bring forward the idea of their having interconnectedness within a larger global society. But now, and for most people, their concerns will be mainly about becoming freed from the tyranny of exploitation by multinational corporations. People want to be free on a one-by-one personal level from this exploitation.

Look at the people of the Middle East. Their psychology is not of a capitalist mentality. They do not want corporate exploitation. They react and cling to their fundamentalism, and the fundamentalists take dominance because the people don't want to be dominated by the capitalists. If instead they can see a solution that is not capitalist, that incorporates their religion's valuing of family and community, and that gives importance to local economic autonomy, they will embrace it. They will jump on these ideas and will give up their fundamentalism for this approach because they want to survive. Everyone wants to survive. So, emphasizing the development of community, family, local economic autonomy, and of world coordination based on the welfare of all living beings—this is what is to be emphasized.

Naturally, some people will react to this vision. They may say it is world tyranny. When responding to the idea of a strong warrior society, a traditional capitalist will call it tyranny, a traditional intellectual will call it tyranny. Why? Because such a society does not support the individual economic approach of the capitalist, nor does it support the individual intellectual or religious approach of the intellectuals. Rather, it supports duty, honor, and collective welfare. The people in dominance in one age are never comfortable with the ascending values of the new age. But the rolling of the ages cannot be changed.

## Defect of Steady State Economics

There are those who want to minimize the use of resources, and they believe that the earth's carrying capacity is fixed and finite and that we can therefore only have a fixed population and no economic growth. They hold an assumption that we have a fixed resource base to live on—a certain amount of oil, timber, food, etc.

But is it so? Is there only a certain amount of solar energy, a certain amount of mental creativity? Their assumptions take too material of a perspective. The assumption is being made that technology will not progress. But technology will go forward. Pollution and environmental degradation occur because technology has not sufficiently developed; it is still primitive. When our technology becomes more sophisticated, and its development is guided by concern for the environment, it will not have the ecologically destructive impacts that is does today.

However, more developed technology will be more dangerous, so the society will need to be more regulated because the same technology that can create survival can also be destructive. Without a strongly regulated society, much advanced technology is highly dangerous. Already there are technologies that are at a dangerous stage in our present under-regulated society.

People are not ready for the level of regulation that is required, but they are beginning to see that there is a need for regulation. In response, some are advocating what is essentially a highly regulated approach to economic development—that of a steady state economy. But this is a defective approach because it assumes that population will be remain stable and that technology will remain as it is today. Neither of these assumptions are credible, and they make this a faulty theory.

## Controlling Global Population

Of course, we cannot assume that population can continue to grow and that there will always be plenty of food and materials to sustain the growing population. There is truth in the assertion that population has grown beyond of the carrying capacity of the earth and that population has reached a level that is unsustainable. The size of the human population has become disproportionate and has become a blight, bringing the destruction of many species, polluting the earth, and endangering the metabolic functions of the very planet on which we live.

Human population will go down—whether by birth control or other means. The population of most of Europe, much of the Far East is already going down. America is only growing because of immigration. Population naturally diminishes among people with greater technology and a better standard of living. But the population of many poorer nations continues to grow unsustainably because many people in these countries retain the belief that greater numbers of offspring will assure them more security. This type of thinking is from an older time, and it is contributing to the harm of the planet.

There needs to be regulation in the society. The population cannot be sustained even at today's level—not with our present technology and lifestyles. Unfortunately, certain ways of controlling population growth can be quite devastating. If the population continues to overshoot the Earth's resource base there may be harsh consequences.

It is a critical time of shift and change in human history. The economic crisis is but one problem amid many, the most serious being that the earth is being killed. The oceans are dying. The land, sea and air are polluted. Water supplies and water tables are diminishing; the amount of usable water is dwindling. Global warming and shifts in climate are reducing the amount of usable land and increasing weather catastrophes. The earth that civilization has emerged on is endangered.

## Humanity's Future is Bright

The capitalist approach of development for personal need— not taking into account the larger collective good—must change and change quickly. The shift from the capitalist era through popular revolution to a warrior era will be a tumultuous time. A significant change of values is occurring and hanging in the balance is the very survival of human life, and of much other life, on planet earth.

But humanity will rally. There will be difficulty, there will be loss of population, but society will not fall to some primitive level. People will find their way to a coordinated global society with local economic autonomy. Necessity brings solutions. Even now, many begin to see the necessity. They see these destructive forces looming. They see looming great challenges to the human society, to living beings, to the planet earth.

It is a time of turmoil, but the future of humanity is bright. There are those who predict that humanity will not survive. But PROUTists' answer is that the future of humanity is bright, and that people's quality of life will get better.

Not all will make it through this transition. There will be calamities; there will be a natural reduction in the human population. But a great transition is occurring; society is coming of age. It is becoming a global society. It is becoming an interconnected world, having an immediate need to address the global needs of humanity and of the planet. For this, we must, on one hand, encourage local economic development, and, on the other hand, we must encourage global responsibility and a coordinated global society.

# 10

# Restoring Balance in Society

The dominant approach to economic development has equated social progress with economic growth. But economic growth, as an end in itself, has become like a cancer disrupting the healthy functioning of communities and of ecosystems. In making material increase the measure of social and individual good, there comes to be alienation from deeper purpose and meaning in human life. Moreover, economic growth is now so out of balance with the resource base and the ecological balances of the planet as to be unsustainable—it is now estimated that it would take 1.8 planet Earths to provide the resources needed to sustain humanity at its present level of resource consumption.

Critics of growth have put forward alternatives. These alternatives are variations on the themes of so-called sustainable development or of abandoning growth in favor of a steady-state economy. Neither of these options has proven popular. The call for slowing or stopping growth has been opposed by developing societies in particular, as they feel a pressing need to rapidly increase their economic output to meet the basic needs of their populations, while people of the developed world remain addicted to growing affluence. As for sustainable development, it has been criticized as being vague as an operational concept, or as being a continuation of unsustainable growth dressed up to appear environmentally responsible.

PROUT does not advocate limiting growth and has not attempted to define what constitutes sustainable development as such, but instead puts emphasis on establishing balance, on seeking equilibrium of social processes. This equilibrium applies not only to economic activity but is a comprehensive balance, affecting all spheres of life in an integrated manner. So, all three spheres of life—material, psychic, and spiritual —are developed in a balanced way, and then all three are balanced together as a whole.

The concept of balance reflects ecological processes; it mirrors in human society the dynamic balancing of biological processes that occurs in the natural world. Humanity is not separate from nature but is an extension, a part, of it. Human society functions best when upholding nature's principles, and this requires maintaining equilibrium in all spheres of human expression.

Human society, while not separate from broader natural processes, does have its uniqueness, as human nature includes the potential for spiritual expression. It is our spiritual urge that best provides a context for measuring social progress. Social progress should not be defined as the mere increase in material abundance, but as the collective movement toward material and psychological conditions that provide a congenial environment for spiritual development.

## Three Stages in the Loss of Balance

If a society is to grow and flourish, it must have balance. There must be balance in collective life so that the physical, psychological, and spiritual needs of the individuals within the society will be met. If there is not balance, then in some sphere or spheres the needs of human beings will not be met, and when this occurs, if the imbalance goes deep and is not rectified, the collective welfare plummets toward a dismal fate. When human needs are suppressed, when members of the society are oppressed, the overall collective suffers. Eventually the effect may become so great that the society will collapse. Maintaining balance within the collective sphere is very important for the development of a healthy society in which all people may grow and flourish, in which they may come to live as true human beings.

The progressive loss of balance in the society has three stages. First is *derangement*, which occurs when in the psychic sphere people's thinking becomes imbalanced. For example, if due to materialism, people develop a greedy outlook and think that the natural world is merely for exploitation by human beings, that it exists for our use. This outlook is a derangement of thought. In a society in which the thinking is deranged in this fashion, it is hard for a person to grasp an understanding of the oneness of being. An attitude of human privilege will dominate the collective psyche, and an individual will have to struggle to realize their inherent unity with all life. So, concepts which are collectively accepted but do not support reality—this stage is derangement in the collective sphere. It is the first stage in the society's loss of balance.

If this derangement is allowed to continue and defective thinking is not corrected, then destructive actions will result from these thoughts. The environment will get destroyed for the sake of human greed, and the actions of exploitative persons will dominate the overall direction in which the society progresses. When this happens, there comes to be *disruption*—the second stage in the loss of balance. No longer do the people live in balance with their natural surroundings, no longer do they conduct their collective life according to the natural laws, but there becomes a disruption in the workings of the society.

The faulty thinking at this stage gets manifested in the actions of people. The society becomes fragmented. Exploitation of one group over another becomes prominent. Greed is often rampant. The animals are abused in the greedy grasping of people whose clarity of mind has been lost. These lost souls do not even know the tragedy of their plight. They are unaware of their foolishness. Such a society becomes disrupted in all spheres of its functioning, and for people living in such a world it becomes difficult to grasp their spiritual essence. They are led astray from the course of social development that would lead them towards spiritual life.

If the stage of disruption continues to afflict a society over time, its functioning cannot be maintained. It is only a matter of time before a society in which the thinking is deranged and people's vital nature is disrupted falls into *degeneration*—the third stage in the loss of balance. When this occurs, not only are people's actions corrupted but they become self-defeating, self-destructive. Society becomes degenerated to the point that action in every sphere becomes harsh and destructive. All will suffer and many will die.

Whole cultures have collapsed in this fashion. Social life cannot be supported if it does not have some basic measure of balance with the operative forces of nature. If sufficient disparity is there, degeneration and annihilation become inevitable. Then, out of the ashes of collapsed social order, a new healthy society may be built in which human beings may realize their potentiality in all spheres and live a life that affords them opportunity to realize their human purpose.

## Restoring Balance

While societies that reach the stage of degeneration typically fall into collapse, this fate is not inevitable. A reversal of the loss of balance is possible. However, it is not an easy task to restore balance to a society which has degenerated. First of all, there must be a revival of a social structure in which people may regain their dignity and their integrity. To develop this, there must be a spiritual base established, and then there must be the proper education of the masses, particularly the youth.

People must be inspired. They cannot be forced to change; they cannot be led in a totalitarian manner; they cannot be pushed about. Even if the intent is good, such an approach will ultimately lead to failure and will bring social progress. For progress there must be an approach which emphasizes the development of people. Give the people inspiration, give them hope, give them vitality. Inspire them to rise up. Bring out their innate nature. Do not order them about and impose rules; this approach will not bring a new society.

The road from degeneration back to balance must start with nurturing inspiration so that the spirit of people is renewed, and they are restored to their original state, to their fundamental nature, and are given scope to express their inherent nature in the society. This is not achieved through political movements, nor is it done through totalitarian rule. If through revolutionary struggle control of the government is gained and the people are forced to change, it will be a failure. It must be done through inspiration; people must be inspired. Give them back their hope, their dignity, their humanity. Give them education. These are the forces that change society. Only when the people have risen up can the social order be changed. And when the social order is changed, there will naturally come a change in the leadership.

The process of restoring balance is not done through political rule, rather political rule is purified through the restoration of balance. This must be remembered or else a faulty strategy may be taken which leads to failure. Appeal must be made to the hearts and minds of people. Give them back their dignity, give them back their autonomy, give them hope. Give them a way to know themselves, to know the greatness that is within them and to express their inner greatness in the world.

When the restoration of people's connection to their essential human nature happens, balance will automatically be restored, and corrupt and oppressive political systems will inevitably collapse. For spiritually vital people cannot be oppressed, cannot be corrupted. They will dynamically work to change the society because their spirits are alive. And when there is a collective awakening, defective social and political systems will become responsive; they will certainly be forced to change.

When restoring balance in a society there must be a step-by-step methodical approach which renews vitality, restores hope, and gives human beings the means to know and express the divinity within them. To inspire people and give them access to their divine nature is the best method to empower them to devote themselves to restoring balance.

# 11

# Humanity Is at a Crossroads

Humanity is at a crossroads. On one hand is the path of our sure destruction and of the significant destruction to the planet that sustains us. The speed of this path to destruction is now increasing even beyond the expectations of the concerned environmental scientists.

In the face of this growing destruction, the political leaders act as if their hands are tied. And they are—either by political infighting or by unresponsive bureaucracies. But, more importantly, they lack the political will to bring change. There are the resources for change; the wealth to fund the needed changes exists. But this wealth is in the hands of a few—the billionaires and the multi-millionaires who gain their wealth mainly from their investments in multinational corporations. The political leaders are too beholden to these wealthy elites and know that there is only so far that they can go in making demands on them.

The present economic system is digging away at its own foundations and is becoming more and more unstable. Societies are choking on their own pollution. The waves of refugees who need food, clothing, shelter and jobs are steadily growing. The homeless people on the city streets of America are urban refugees occupying encampments even in the wealthiest American cities. The inequities caused by capitalism's deficient systems are increasingly coming to the fore.

There are leaders who are basically good people and who have the potential to govern for the good of the citizens, but they cannot prevail against the wealthy corporations and individuals who are addicted to increasing their profits and wealth. People are struggling to get and keep a job, to pay for housing and food, but the conditions caused by the wealth addiction of the rich have caught them in its web.

Many people have an aversion to discomforting truths. But these discomforting truths cannot be avoided. Take the truth of climate change. As weather disasters grow, it is increasingly hard to avoid the truth that climate change is human caused. Yet, people keep burning hydrocarbons even as they suffer from the growing weather disasters.

Capitalism is eating itself from the inside, but as its erosion is internal its precarious condition is not so visible. That is why capitalism will end in sudden collapse. The Soviet Union quickly crumbled under its own weight, but capitalism will explode. It will go down suddenly, like a building whose foundations have weakened from internal corrosion until it abruptly collapses.

While capitalism may end in shambles, people will still need goods and services for their daily lives. The need for an economy will still be there, but with the failure of the capitalist system, new conditions will exist, and new opportunities will open up. Cooperatives producing basic necessities and small farms and agricultural communities will be able to flourish. Innovators, repairers, distributors, renovators, and small businesses meeting human needs will all do well in the absence of the choking suck of capitalism. Money will stay in circulation, or new forms of exchange will be created, and the economy will regenerate quickly, taking a new form.

## Spreading the Seeds of a New System

The current economic system requires ever increasing consumption to hold it up—consumption at levels that are unsustainable. When this consumption driven system stops, the current economy will stop. The new economy that will succeed it will need to be built on commerce in necessities and basic amenities, and not superfluous goods. Out of necessity humanity will have to adopt economies based on PROUT-like approaches, and these economies will be grounded in the values of neohumanism. That is, the well-being of human beings and of the earth's living beings will come first.

The approaches and values of a PROUT system were first conceived some time ago, and its seeds are now ready to be spread. Some seeds have already been planted in demonstration projects and placed in books, articles, and videos. Some are held in the minds of progressive individuals. But these seeds cannot fully sprout as yet as the rich soil of human innovation, commitment, and drive is so adversely impacted by the domineering grip of capitalism. But when capitalism is gone, then the fertile earth and the creative human minds will have plenty of rich soil and energy with which to build a new society.

We cannot easily imagine how change will occur and what it will be like on the other side of this great shift, for at present the tendrils of capitalism limit our thinking and choke off progressive change. Consider how it has pervaded the utilization of the

Internet.

Capitalism will fall and we must be ready—not for disaster but for opportunity. Progressive forces are already hard at work creating opportunities for the dispersal of new ideas and new approaches. They are building the foundations of the new society, though as yet little can be seen of their work. They are going forward, knowing—those who see deeply enough—that soon the conditions of the world will change and the demand for their knowledge and vision will keep them busy.

The problem that the advocates of a new society are now facing is that the tentacles of capitalism are sucking the lifeblood and energies of people everywhere, and so their message is not heard above the noise. But after an earthquake, when everything is reduced to rubble, the sound of one helicopter bringing relief aid is a very loud and welcome noise. This is how it will be: those with a progressive vision will be like the relief workers after the earthquake, bringing what is necessary to rebuild the society upon the rubble of what was.

The infrastructure of the corporate economy which people have come to rely on will be gone, so new cooperative enterprises will have to be launched quickly. Work opportunities and purchasing power will have to be created to address suffering and get goods and services flowing. When capitalism has gone to ashes, out of the ashes the phoenix of a people's economy can rise.

When the Soviet Union fell there was widespread suffering. But, as we saw, people are resilient. The farms still produced food, though the distribution of the food was disorganized. Electricity and fuel were still produced, though there were no innovative systems established for rational distribution. The bureaucrats and police still showed up for work, though their paychecks were disrupted. The buses ran and the airplanes flew, though the service was basic. Consumer goods were scarce, yet there were enough necessities and amenities available for people to survive.

What was not there when Soviet communism collapsed was innovative thinking on a new direction. No one had a better system to put in its place; there was no progressive vision. So, capitalists from the global economy and local opportunists rushed in and purchased the resources for pennies on the ruble. Opportunists flourished and fed on the misery of the people. A class of multimillionaires quickly formed and became a cabal of quasi-capitalist oligarchs, accumulating wealth among a few while the post-Soviet society as a whole languished.

But now, with capitalism's collapse there will be PROUT, built on the value base of neohumanism, and there will be the many progressive ideas and models that are compatible with PROUT's synthetic economic framework. So, the potential for a progressive vision now exists to replace capitalism. Only the progressive minded society builders must be ready to spring into action—like the disaster action teams of the relief organizations following a great catastrophe—and they must also have the political strength to see that greed driven opportunists can't consolidate a grip on society's resources to form a Russian-like oligarchy.

## The Time for Planning is Now

PROUTists and their many allies must make their post-collapse action plans now and have all in readiness for when the opportunity strikes. As with Soviet communism, capitalism's fall will happen very fast, and in the devastation of its fall people will be listening for the sound of the relief helicopter, bringing knowledge of how to reorganize their local economies so they will have food to eat and cooperative businesses to work in and purchasing power to obtain their necessities and the other requisites to rebuild a life for themselves and their families.

People's homes or their neighborhoods will need gardens, solar or wind powered energy generating systems, and supplies of potable water. Clean sources of heat and fuel will be needed. Ride sharing and public transport will become the norm, for the cost of individual auto ownership will become unaffordable to most. Repair and renovation of existing mechanical systems will flourish, for the engines of mass production will be paused for lack of demand and loss of investment. Newly structured local governing boards will need to be formed to supersede the old non-functional governing systems.

Most of all, people will need a workable vision and the practical blueprints to build the new economic and political systems. All of this is contained in PROUT, built on the value base of neohumanism.

It is likely that the capitalist economy will fall faster than did the Soviet Union's communist economy. But if PROUT-like vision and practical solutions can be brought forward swiftly, capitalism's replacement will be fast, and the new system will arise quickly.

So, the progressive visionaries need to prepare themselves by learning the practical aspects of how to operate the economic and governing systems based on neohumanism-guided approaches. Teams of society rejuvenating responders should be trained on every level. And they should begin now building demonstration projects, for these will become very important in the near future. These PROUT-inspired models must be easy and quick to build and be readily replicable.

In many places in the aftermath of capitalism's fall there may be a need to rapidly construct temporary shelters for the unhoused while they begin their new jobs and build their new lives. In some places, with the complicating impacts of climate change disasters, flooded, burned or demolished cities and towns will have to be abandoned wholesale and new self-sustaining towns and livable cities will have to be quickly built to replace them. These new settlements, if built on the inspiration of PROUT's integrated development schemes, will flourish.

Non-polluting sources of energy will have to be quickly created to provide for the energy needs of the world's peoples. Following capitalism's collapse, during the transition, energy sources will not be plentiful. However, with rational and innovative utilization of resources, there can be enough for all—just not enough for wasteful use by a few.

So, the new economic and governing vision must be brought forward at the proper time, and that time is quickly approaching. The time is now to actively prepare. It is time to lay down the backbone of the distribution of knowledge of the application of PROUT-like social system so that a new vision and new approaches can flow freely at the time of the quickly approaching apocalypse.

Capitalism has been digging away at its own foundations, and it has no contingency plans for its own collapse. Capitalism will fall. And the few remnants of communism will also fall, as will the fundamentalism-based governing systems. Outdated governments and economic systems will not be able to function. However, as happened in the aftermath of the Soviet collapse, people will still show up for work, for work is vital to their equilibrium. But they will need new ideas and new hope to guide and inspire their work.

The moment of great change is coming. We must prepare to seize the day.

# Appendix

# The Social Cycle

PROUT has brought forward a new theory of history—called the *social cycle*—in which there is a cyclic rotation of class dominance involving four social classes: workers, warriors, intellectuals and entrepreneurs. As the social cycle is referred to in this book, a brief explanation of it is given below.

## Collective Psychology

An explanation of the social cycle begins with the concept of *collective psychology*. Humanity's ideas, urges, and sentiments undergo continuous change, and out of these psychic changes flow the changing currents of history. History is the multi-faceted expression of the people of a society, which is generated by their collective psychology.

Collective psychology is defined as the aggregate psychic expression of a people that results from their shared views, values, and desires. Collective psychology is the overall psychic approach of a people; it's their combined mentality that forms their core beliefs.

Whenever there is a group of people gathered together for some time, they will begin to develop a set of beliefs and opinions that they collectively share. And when others join and assimilate into that group, they also will come to accept the same set of principles and beliefs that collective group has developed. This is the influence of the collective psychology. Collective psychology is bound to exist whenever there is any extended group association, be it ten people or ten million people.

Causality in history—the direction of collective motivity—arises from the expression of collective psychology.

## Social Class

The collective psychology of a society's dominant social class has a strong influence on the social expression and historical development of a society. The Viking warrior class imparted to Nordic society characteristics of spiritedness, adventurousness, and conquest. The Buddhist priestly class in Tibet, by contrast, shaped a religion-oriented outlook on life. And in Britain's Victorian era the dominant entrepreneurial class put economic enterprise at the center of national life.

Class dominance is not static but is characterized by a rotation of elites into and out of power. With the inception of the Middle Ages, the clergy replaced the Roman army as the preeminent power in Western Europe. The burghers, in turn, replaced the clergy as the prevailing force in European Renaissance society. And Tito's guerrilla forces brought to an end the grip of the moneyed class in Yugoslavia and gave rise to a new militarist dominant culture.

The movement of social classes in and out of dominance follows a cyclic pattern; one class after another comes into prominence in a regular order of succession (as described below). But this movement is not always fluid, the natural progression of class rule is often obstructed. This occurs because there is a tendency for the dominant class to become entrenched. It then becomes oppressive toward the other classes, and when this occurs the fluid movement of class rotation becomes stuck and society stagnates.

Orthodox Marxists believe that the solution to class oppression is to create a classless society. However, this approach is bound to be futile, as the existence of classes is a natural phenomenon. Instead of attempting to suppress the existence of classes, class oppression can be overcome by facilitating the cyclic flow of class succession, that is, by advancing the social cycle in its natural progression and not allowing it to become stuck in the grip of entrenched class interests. Class dominance may be inevitable, but class oppression is not.

PROUT considers class oppression to be the central problem of human history and gives much attention to its practical resolution. Before going into this subject, it will be helpful to first understand PROUT's conception of social class.

The concept of social class provides us with a way of looking at social differentiation or stratification. There are several ways in which social theorists have conceptualized class. Most contemporary sociological concepts of class are based on measures of power, wealth and social status. Marxist sociology, however, defines class on the basis of people's relationship to the system of production—the most significant classes in Marxist class typology being the owners of production and the laborers they employ.

PROUT's class typology is derived from four deep psychological orientations to life, each of which gives rise to a particular social class. The four social classes are:

- laborers, whose orientation is toward their work and physical enjoyment,

- warriors, whose orientation is toward valor and physical challenge,
- intellectuals, whose orientation is toward intellect and creativity, and
- entrepreneurs, whose orientation is toward creating and acquiring wealth.

Each of these classes has its characteristic style of collective expression, and the style of expression of the dominant class characterizes the society they dominate. Societies may differ one from another in many respects, but if they have the same class in dominance, they will tend to have some fundamental characteristics in common. Ancient warrior societies in India, China, Africa, Europe and the Americas, for example, all had disciplined social structures under a monarch or chieftain, with their predominant social values being those of honor, valor, loyalty, social duty and bravery.

Individuals express one of the four mental styles of relating to the world—laborer, warrior, intellectual and entrepreneur—and their characteristic mental style will determine the social roles that are natural to their psychic expression. A person with warrior tendency of mind, for example, may become a police officer, fire fighter, army soldier, mountain climber or gang member—but is unlikely end up a corporate executive, scientific researcher or migrant laborer.

Unlike other concepts of class, the PROUT concept is not dependent upon the social values or upon the conditions of a particular culture or era. It is a system of class based solely on tendencies of mind that are universal. Because this class system is universal, it is applicable to all societies and all times, providing cross-cultural usefulness in understanding the patterns of class dynamics that occur in human history.

## The Social Cycle

There is a cyclic pattern to the succession into dominance of the social classes. P. R. Sarkar termed this rotating pattern the *social cycle*. The social cycle's natural progression is from laborer class to warrior class to intellectual class to entrepreneurial class. This sequence of class dominance then repeats.

The social cycle started with the labor class in dominance. The first humans were preoccupied with meeting their physical needs. This preoccupation with survival created in them a laborer mentality, and this mentality shaped the nature of their society.

Laborer society was largely guided by the immediate demands of their environment. People lived in groups maintained out of mutual need for self-protection and a sharing of labor. Mating relationships had little permanence and were often polyandrous. Family ties typically centered around the maternal instincts that bonded mothers to their children.

The hard lives of these early humans were challenging and focused on their basic material needs. While they had craft, art and stories that expressed their humanity, they had little opportunity to develop subtler aspects of mind. They were awed by the powerful forces of nature around them, and much of their religious feelings were oriented toward propitiating deities they associated with these forces.

## Warrior Era

Over time, increasing numbers in the laborer society ceased to face the world with passivity and fear but looked upon the obstacles and dangers of their environment as challenges to confront and conquer. They developed character traits of courage, valor, and spiritedness. Those who possessed this warrior mentality assumed dominance over the laborers, and the rise of a warrior society took place.

The early warriors lived to express strength, courage and vitality through fight and conquest. Because of their high-spiritedness they developed a strong sense of honor. Their warrior code of honor carried such importance to them that a noble death was preferable to ignoble defeat or dishonorable conduct.

Because of their concern with prestige, they felt a sense of conscience and duty. This had a healthy effect on society; out of duty, warrior men took greater responsibility for their families and women were less burdened with being the providers and protectors of the young. Eventually, socially recognized marriage came into practice.

At the beginning of the warrior era, leadership was matriarchal, with powerful women accepted as the group mothers of their tribal societies. Matriarchal rule was humanity's first governing system. Matriarchy was eventually replaced by the rule of male chieftains. Although women lost their place as leaders, they generally enjoyed social respect comparable to men's, and in some tribal arrangements it was the women elders who selected the chieftains.

Warriors remembered and glorified the valiant deeds of their ancestors. For this reason, they placed importance on family heritage. Respect for family led warrior children to feel a sense of duty towards their parents, and family ties became strengthened. With the formation of tight family units, society too became more unified.

Unlike the laborers, the warriors' religious expression was not motivated by awe of the forces of nature; rather, it reflected a fearless and high-minded mentality. When they prayed, they asked their gods to provide for their subjects. The deities they prayed to were powerful animal spirits or human-like gods and goddesses having qualities glorified in the warrior society. While animism and polytheism were the common forms of religious expression, this era also saw early development of monotheistic and mystical beliefs.

The warring nature of their society required a high degree of social unity and discipline, which bound kingdoms together with efficient systems of social administration and coordinated transport and communication systems. These led to the origins of the state as an institution in society.

After the warrior society adopted patriarchal rule, leadership was typically held by a chieftain who established his right to lead through superior physical might. With the death of a chieftain, the strongest warrior would make claim to succession. If leadership was contested, it might be determined through battle. To put an end to the destructiveness of these conflicts, in most places a hereditary system of succession was eventually adopted.

Because of the power and daring of great monarchs, the laborers looked upon them with awe and submitted to their rule. The kings, in turn, felt obliged to protect their subjects. But the rule of these absolute monarchs was not always paternal and benevolent. They often wielded power callously for the sake of their own glory. When they lusted after increasing territory and stature, their subjects were conscripted to fight in their wars of conquest. They built up their empires without concern for the toll of lives lost in battle.

Through the system of hereditary succession to the throne, leadership was often passed on to unworthy descendants who became monarchs by virtue of royal birth but lacked the qualities of heroic bravery and high-spiritedness. Leadership in the warrior society was then weakened, foreshadowing the downfall of the warrior class.

A second factor also led to the warriors' loss of supremacy. Warrior leaders possessed courage and strength, but most lacked the intellect required to devise tactics of warfare, invent weaponry, or efficiently administer vast and complex empires. As a result, they became increasingly dependent upon people with intellect to advise and assist them. Gradually, their ministers and councilors assumed ever-greater influence in the affairs of society and state.

## Intellectual Era

In advanced warrior empires, there was a growth of a class of people employed in intellectual work. Not only did their numbers increase, but their power as well. The dull-witted, pseudo-warrior royalty lacked the astuteness to perceive the cunning of the aspiring intellectual class. Almost without being aware of it, the proud royalty had their power wrested from them by shrewd councilors and clergy. Kings became puppets to their ministers; the system of rule was no longer genuine monarchy but became a "ministocracy." Under ministocracy the locus of power shifted, but the outer form of government remained unchanged. The ministers were the power behind the throne, but they kept the facade of monarchy as a convenient means to control the commoners, who believed their kings ruled by divine right.

A new era dawned in which society was dominated by the intellectual class. In the early phase of the intellectual era, society benefited to some extent. The intelligentsia introduced a more orderly social system, and they often saved the common people from the monarch's arbitrary high-handedness and from the cruel slavery to which many had been subjected.

Intellectuals do not feel impotent in the face of obstacles. But neither do they leap into struggle, as do the warriors. They instead use their keen intellect to first conceive a plan of action; then they implement this strategy using the physical labor of the workers and the brute force and courage of the warriors. It is an approach to action characterized by thoughtfulness and cunning.

Those who are mentally evolved have the capacity to direct their psyches towards high-mindedness and spiritual awareness. But the ruling intellectuals were rarely motivated by benevolence and spirituality. Most used their mental abilities to fulfill sensual desires, and they acquired the objects of their desire without taking physical risk or performing hard labor but by exploiting the laborers and warriors.

The intellectuals were adept at making an outward show of honesty and piousness. But to maintain dominance and gratify their passions they were fully capable of unscrupulous actions. Because of their cunning, it was difficult to discern their sinister intentions. Unlike the warriors, whose path is simple and straightforward, the intellectuals were masters of deceit. Both the ambitiousness and the callousness of the intelligentsia often exceeded that of the power-thirsting monarchs of the warrior era.

Unlike the warriors, the intellectuals could not bully others around through brute force. So, they devised other methods to compel people to do their bidding. The intellectual clergy would cloud people's minds with religious dogmas, illogical superstitions, and mythological stories. These were propagated to instill fears and inferiority complexes in the minds of the masses. The clergy created fear in people through the threat of suffering in the eternal fires of hell, should they fail to keep blind adherence to religious dogma. The minds of common people were filled with bigotry, fanaticism, and blind faith. This led to some of the darkest chapters in human history. It was not possible for the uneducated people of the Middle Ages to conceive of defying the God-sanctioned authority of the popes, ayatollahs, and high priests. Even mighty kings became compliant servants of the Church.

The intellectual era also had a constructive side. To maintain their position, the priesthood found it expedient to preach religious ideas. The sermons they delivered inspired common people to take up moral and spiritual development. And to impress others with their piety, the clergy undertook public service. All this had a healthy effect on social development.

There was yet another good that came from the intellectuals' rule. Due to their talent for effective administration, the potentialities of the people were put to fuller use. The material base of the society thus increased, and, in general, people could better obtain their basic necessities. People also enjoyed a greater security. Instead of the state being run by royal whim—as in the warrior age—government was run through systems of law and codified authority.

But the society of the intellectual era was not built out of concern for human sentiments. This was evident in the institution of marriage. The families of the betrothed boy and girl made marriage arrangements without regard for the children's feelings, their primary interest being to maintain family prestige and preserve the rigidity of the class system.

Women were severely oppressed in the intellectual era. They lost all human dignity and were made wageless slaves and objects of men's enjoyment. The church concocted scriptural injunctions, presented as divine commandments, declaring that women's role is to bear children and serve her husband. Because of this oppressive dogma, women's very existence was defined in relation to men. Without a husband and children, their lives held little meaning in the eyes of society. This caused women to develop crippling inferiority complexes and to suffer lives of anguish and despair.

In short, the society of the intellectual era paid little regard to humanity. The religious dogmas were severely rigid, and the social institutions were oppressive and inhumane.

But not all mentally developed people of that era were social parasites. There were also noble-minded individuals who bravely struggled to humanize the social system. Great spiritual teachers—such as Chaitanya Mahaprabhu, Milarepa, Hildegard of Bingen, Francis of Assisi, and Meister Eckhart—sought to awaken humanity to the thrill of freedom, universal love, and dogma-free thinking. These saintly personalities were dearly loved by the common people but viciously attacked by those having privileged interests to protect. While the ruling intellectuals obstinately opposed the reformers, once their progressive ideas gained popular acceptance, the defenders of orthodoxy hypocritically praised their greatness.

## Entrepreneurial Era

In the intellectual era, material wealth gradually assumed greater importance, and the nobility and clergy indulged heavily in the acquisition and enjoyment of refined material objects, such as works of art, finely crafted luxuries, and lavish manors and churches. Their refined tastes required financing. They also required financing for their war campaigns and crusades. Though they desired material wealth, and money to provision their armies, they had little aptitude for trade, capital accumulation, expanding markets or money lending.

It is the entrepreneurial class that is adept at these commercial activities, and the intelligentsia eventually found themselves dependent on the merchants and financiers. As this dependence grew, they were no longer able to maintain their position of social dominance, and they were compelled to offer up their formidable intellectual abilities into the service of those who controlled the economy. Thus, the entrepreneurial class, through the force of wealth, came to dominate the nobility, clergy and professionals— as well as the military and the workers. A new era began, one in which the society became controlled by the capitalists.

The capitalist age first emerged in Europe in the post-Medieval Era. It began with the rapidly rising influence of powerful banking houses and the urban bourgeois. It was also stimulated by the era of exploration and discovery and the increase in trade that followed contact with new lands. During this early period, the entrepreneurial class replaced the stagnant, feudal economy with mercantilism. Later, the laissez-faire economic system was introduced. At about the same time as the advent of the laissez-faire economy came the industrial revolution. By this time, the entrepreneurial class enjoyed unchallenged dominance in nearly all of Europe, and their immense economic power spanned much of the globe.

With the capitalist era came the rise of nationalism. Underlying the patriotic fervor of nationalism was the capitalists' quest to gain strategic control over resources and to protect and extend their markets. Political and economic imperialism was an inevitable outgrowth of nationalism. Imperialism led to the enslavement of colonized peoples, and it created a dangerous threat to global peace and unity. The rivalries among imperialist powers for access to resources and markets were a main cause of wars. Imperialism also brought the imposition of capitalist dominance over most non-industrialized societies of the world.

Whereas intellectuals enjoy material objects through their use, capitalists enjoy wealth more through its possession. Their drive is to accumulate wealth, not necessarily to utilize it. Whereas intellectuals acquired riches while maintaining an appearance of piety, capitalists amassed wealth in an open and straightforward manner.

Capitalists can exhibit great courage in their bold initiatives to increase their wealth. They bravely face the ups and downs in their fortune, and they take big risks as they gamble their capital on opportunities for greater gain. But, unlike the warriors, capitalists are not constrained by a sense of honor in their struggles. Their empire building is undertaken without scruples or inhibition from moral codes. For the sake of obtaining money, they are willing to compromise their character and ignore the wellbeing of society and environment.

There are, of course, some in the capitalist class who possess a conscience and who are charitable. Many engage in philanthropy, often influenced by religious beliefs. But however charitable may be their motivation for giving, they usually enjoy a return on their philanthropy through enhancement of their public image.

When the money-minded outlook of the capitalists becomes predominant, the social value of the individual gets assessed in monetary terms, and the social status that individuals command depends mostly on their financial worth. Money buys respect.

The capitalist-dominated society generally retains the system of male supremacy created in the intellectual era. For the most part, women remain deprived of full social status and are economically dependent on men. However, capitalism exhibits greater flexibility on gender issues, as women make for both talented workers and good consumers. In the recent phase of the capitalist era, liberalizing reforms have brought women legal equality in most nations, though less progress has been made in removing their second-class economic status.

In the capitalist era, the political system underwent substantial change. The moneyed class found that theocratic or monarchical rule was not responsive enough to their interests, so they preferred the democratic government. Under democracy, the electorate is easily swayed by political leaders' promises and propaganda. The politicians, in turn, are well aware of their dependence on big campaign contributions and on the need for capitalists to support, or at least not be threatened by, their legislative agendas.

Democracy, however, is not always the most effective system for governing, as it can be unwieldy or ineffective when there is too much factionalized party politics. And it can get in the way if mass social unrest threatens capitalist rule. So, democracy sometimes gets replaced by dictatorship or by military rule. Because capitalist-dominated societies may have either democratic or dictatorial rule, it can be difficult to discern if a country is in its capitalist era just by looking at its form of government. That is, by outward appearances, a capitalist society can appear to be a warrior dominated society.

There is one indicator which can often be used to analyze whether a country is under capitalist domination: Under capitalist rule, while either professional administrators or military generals may run the government, an orthodox capitalist will almost always control the treasury. Governmental positions such as minister of finance, chair of the national bank, or secretary of the treasury are held by influential members of the capitalist class.

Intellectuals play a vital role in the capitalists' socioeconomic system. Their professional skills are essential for operating a society in which the capitalist economy can grow and function with little opposition. Legislators frame laws advantageous to the propertied class. Diplomats negotiate trade agreements that protect corporate interests. Journalists write news reports conforming to the pro-business slant of publishers. Industrial psychologists devise more efficient production systems. Political scientists and economists articulate sophisticated justifications for capitalism. Artists and actors provide advertising images to stimulate consumption or culture to distract the populace. Technicians and scientists invent new products to increase corporate profits. And administrators maintain the efficient control of the social, educational and economic institutions.

The courage and might of the warrior class are also employed to further capitalist interests. The police are called on to suppress militant social unrest, and military forces are sent to quell popular revolutionary movements or protect the capitalists' geopolitical interests. Political leaders will rally public support for these military interventions, claiming they are needed to protect democracy. But usually it is the economic interests of big banks and corporations that are being protected.

For their bravery, military heroes are honored with medals and official praise. For their brilliant accomplishments, intellectuals are awarded prizes and titles. Having been rewarded with a little money or reputation, the warriors and intellectuals continue in their loyal service. Some may recognize that they are prostituting their talents, but they accept their role out of self-interest, lack of socioeconomic consciousness, or their need to earn a living.

This acquiescence, however, is not universal. There are many moral-minded intellectuals and warriors who speak out against exploitation, injustice, and ecological destruction. But there are risks to be had in openly opposing capitalism. Additionally, the pervasive influence of capitalist ideology makes it difficult to analyze the deep causes of social problems. Under ordinary conditions, the number of people who oppose capitalist rule generally remains few.

By marshaling capital and the productive capacities of intellectuals, warriors, and laborers entrepreneurs have brought a great burst of technological and material advancement. During the capitalist era, there has been an unparalleled rise in material abundance. But most capitalist societies are also afflicted by great disparities in wealth, rampant exploitation and desperate poverty. In addition, the earth has been subjected to alarming ecological damage.

Greed-driven capitalists do not view the human society as a living entity to be nurtured, but as a resource to inflate their wealth. Rather than functioning in symbiotic unity with the other elements of society, capitalists parasitically exploit the vital force of others. So intent are they on building their financial empires that they devitalize the very social organism they infest.

## Workers Revolution

When the harmful effects of capitalist greed become severe, mass opposition arises, leading to strikes, demonstrations, and other forms of resistance that threaten the smooth functioning of the capitalist system.

The ruling class then employs efficient means for blunting the force of social protest and protecting the status quo. One of their most effective strategies is to keep people divided so that they don't recognize their common interests and find the unity needed to end oppression. To implement a divide-and-rule strategy, narrow group interests are encouraged, such as racism, religious chauvinism and regionalism. Capitalist elites also patronize the competing political parties, keeping political rivalries active. When stronger measures are necessary, scab workers are recruited to break strikes, and police forces are used to suppress labor, student and ethnic militancy. Through the compelling influence of their money, the moguls of capital can engage the force of the warrior class and the cunning of the intellectual class to keep the populace ignorant, disunited, and suppressed.

But their incessant drive to accumulate wealth fosters problems such as inflation, unemployment and poverty; alienation, cultural decadence and meaningless of life; urban decay, pollution, and environmental destruction; union busting, police brutality and suppression of civil liberties; and interventionist wars in support of client-state dictators. Such unnatural conditions frustrate and oppress people's aspirations to enjoy a good life. If these conditions become intolerable, revolt may break out against capitalist class domination.

In capitalist societies, class relations get reduced to two groups: the capitalists, who control the production and distribution of wealth; and the laborers, warriors, and intellectuals, who are compelled to sell their physical or mental labor. Although the workers, soldiers, and professionals retain their distinctive mental characteristics, from an economic point of view they all become workers. Their collective revolt against capitalist rule is therefore called a "workers revolution."

Many intellectual-minded people become disgruntled with life under capitalism. From their ranks come instigators of change. They may be Latin American priests with a passion for social justice, or mullahs resisting the incursion of economic globalism in Islamic societies, or university students and professors engaged in political activism, or well-educated counter-culture youth that create new cultural or social models that demonstrate alternatives to capitalist values. Warrior-minded people can also become disgruntled, such as disaffected soldiers, forced to fight without honor in wars to protect the economic empires of the capitalists, or spirited individuals who feel a sense of duty to protect the downtrodden.

Those who are of laborer mentality generally lack the boldness, discernment, and idealism necessary to take up revolution. They are more apt to endure their oppressive conditions, concerned mainly for their day-to-day existence. Not until difficulties become acute enough, and prospects for change hopeful enough, do they jump into the fray of struggle.

In order for the workers revolution to break out, it is not enough for social conditions to be unbearably oppressive. The revolutionary forces must also possess a socioeconomic theory that empowers them to understand the causes and envision the solutions to their oppression. They must overcome those beliefs that inhibit them from fighting against exploitation. They must understand that establishing an exploitation-free society through purely electoral means may not be possible so long as money controls the media and the electoral process. And they must conclude that very few among the rich and powerful will be moved by moral appeals to humanize the system that serves them, and that only appropriate use of pressure can help bring social change.

Competent leaders are also essential for the success of the workers revolution. It is not sufficient for leaders to deliver rousing calls to action. They must also be disciplined, moral, sacrificing, persevering, and clear thinking. They must also have a positive vision and a strategy for attaining their vision.

## Second Rotation of the Social Cycle

After the victory of the workers revolution, society passes out of the capitalist era and into the second laborer era. However, people with laborer mentality lack the inclination and aptitude to establish a firm social order in the aftermath of revolution. Immediately following the fall of the capitalist state, there is typically or a period of social pandemonium. This absence of social order is of short duration; it may last a few hours, days or weeks. It ends when warrior-minded leaders of the workers revolution take control of the state and impose order. With the onset of their firm leadership, the second laborer era ends, and the second warrior era begins.

The new warrior-dominated regimes are quick to initiate social and economic reforms. As a result, the society will rapidly attain social equity and the people will enjoy greater economic security. The warrior society may also take up bold collective tasks of exploration and development. In its early phase, much progressive change will occur under the new warrior collective psychology, with its emphasis on collective unity, duty and discipline.

But, over time, the warrior class will inevitably become more preoccupied with its own interests than with promoting the common welfare. However great the second warrior society may become, however impressive the collective achievements, it progressive bearing will begin to wane; benevolent rule will not endure indefinitely.

Eventually, there will be a dialectical evolution in the society that will bring new leadership, and the intellectual class will once again come to the forefront. The newly influential intellectual class will institute progressive change and bring a new round of social dynamism. But their rule will not maintain a progressive dynamism indefinitely, and it too will turn oppressive as the intellectuals come to rule society in their own interests. Then, again, conditions will arise for the advent of the entrepreneurial class to come to the fore.

In this way, one class will follow another in the succession of class dominance. After the second intellectual era will come the second capitalist era. The capitalist collective psychology will again dominate, and capitalist values will again provide the prevailing motive force in society. When capitalist dominance eventually proves overly burdensome, there will come a new period of workers revolution and then human society will advance into a third round of the social cycle.

The social cycle will move in its natural rotation. None can stop it. But if there is a strong influence in the society by those who are spiritual, moral and committed to universal human progress there need not be class oppression. Such people, if positioned in the nucleus of the society, will be able to fluidly advance the social cycle's rotation in a timely manner so that the society can maintain a progressive bearing. One class after another will continue to dominate the society, but none will have scope to become oppressive.

Ronald Logan is the Director of the PROUT Institute. He is the author of *PROUT: A New Paradigm of Development* and is a contributor to *PROUT Magazine.* He was the co-author of the *Plan for the Economic Development of Khabarovsk Krai on the Basis of PROUT.* Logan is also the cofounder and program director of Dharmalaya, a spiritual center in Eugene, Oregon USA. He has contributed classes and courses to the offerings of Transformation Education, many of which feature presentations on PROUT.